Visions for Schools That Teach Psychological Skills

Joseph Strayhorn, M.D.

Psychological Skills Press
Wexford, Pennsylvania

Published by Psychological Skills Press

Author's email: joestrayhorn@gmail.com

ISBN: 978-1-931773-29-4

Table of Contents

Introduction

I've made my living as a child and adolescent psychiatrist, but I've seen a very important part of my work as an educator, teaching the people that come to me the psychological skills that result in happy and productive living. I've had the privilege of working with teachers who have taught psychological skills in schools. I've taught a variety of courses to students, including psychological skills for elementary students and preschoolers, Advanced Placement Statistics for high schoolers, research methods for college students, an undergraduate course in psychotherapy, clinical methods for medical students and psychiatry residents, and workshops for clinicians. I had the great privilege of homeschooling my two daughters. And I've run a telephone tutoring organization whose goals are the teaching of reading and psychological skills. Education has been a daily activity in my life for a long time.

I'm guessing that more will eventually be accomplished for the mental health of populations by educational methods than by medical methods. I'm hoping that some day, very effective teaching of psychological skills in school will prevent a wide range of psychiatric disorders. A professional lifetime (so far) of observing education across a wide range from very successful to very unsuccessful has filled my head with dreams and visions of what could be done in schools. It has been wonderful to implement many of these ideas within my homeschool experience, within my experience with children I've seen clinically, and within the tutoring organization I direct.

This book doesn't undertake the task of proving that various practices are useful, by citing relevant research. To do so would multiply the size of this book many times over. For example, I advocate cultivating and harnessing the skills of older children to tutor younger ones; entire books have been written on this subject. I speak of the power of fantasy rehearsal to enhance skills; books have been written on this. Citing the research relevant to the stages and methods of reading instruction that I outline here could take up a very large volume.

But my aim, as the title suggests, is to create visions – to describe mental images of ways in which education could be tailored so as to promote the very best lives for students and the ones they affect. My hope is that some who read this can make successes of many of these ideas in their schools.

Chapter 1: Why Teach Psychological Skills?

Why education?

Why do we educate children and adolescents? What are we trying to accomplish? Surely to help them gain the skills, abilities, and traits they need to be happy people and to help others to be happy; to care for themselves and for others; to love their fellow human beings as they love themselves. We might add, these are long-term goals, and part of the art of achieving them is the ability to be patient and resilient and to have fortitude when happiness is elusive. The accomplishment of these goals equals mental health. It also equals ethical behavior, and a good life.

What skills?

What should we teach students to do, to attain these goals? Obviously certain academic skills are central to the job of education. But excellent reading ability goes to waste when the reader can't pull himself away from the television. Excellent writing ability goes unused when the writer has no sense of direction or purpose that leads to something worthwhile to say. Excellent mathematics skills can be harmful when the student is not honest enough to report numbers truthfully. Knowledge of science does no good when the scientist is too drunk or too depressed to produce anything worthwhile. There's something missing when communication skill only persuades people to buy what they don't need; or when engineering skill gets devoted only to making more efficient weapons. There's something wrong when society spends a huge fraction of its resources to protect people from one another.

Psychological skills: The missing piece.

Largely missing or underdeveloped in most educational settings are psychological skills, also called character, also called ethics and values, also called social and emotional learning. Here is an outline of such skills:

1. Productivity. Being able to invest sustained effort toward a worthwhile end.

2. Joyousness. Being able to feel good about one's own good choices, the good things others have done, and the blessings of fate.

3. Kindness. Wanting to make other people happy, taking pleasure from helping others be better off, having a sense of conscience that resists making others unhappy.

4. Honesty. Truthfulness, avoidance of deceit.

5. Fortitude. Handling adversity and frustration in a rational way.

6. Good decisions. A: Individual decisions: Going through a systematic mental process to decide the best thing to do. B: Joint decisions or conflict-resolution: deciding

rationally upon a joint plan, with another person or group of people.

7. Nonviolence. Avoiding killing and hurting except as an absolute last resort.

8. Respectful talk. Except when there is a very good reason not to, communicating with others in the least hurtful ways possible.

9. Friendship-building. Meeting people, making friends, enjoying the art of social conversation, building and strengthening relationships over time.

10. Self-discipline. For the sake of accomplishing goals, being willing to pass up pleasure or endure discomfort.

11. Loyalty. Honoring commitments; having a reasonable sense of obligation to people who have earned it.

12. Conservation. Being thrifty, not wasteful, in the use of resources; working toward the nonwasteful and sustainable use of the earth's resources.

13. Self-care. Having good habits of health and safety, including diet, exercise, sleep, drug non-use, accident-prevention. Also being careful about the health and safety of others.

14. Compliance. Promoting the rule of law. Following and obeying rules, and complying with legitimate authority, except when it is unethical to do so.

15. Positive fantasy rehearsal. Not entertaining oneself with fantasies or fictions of cruel, violent, and maladaptive actions, unless there is redeeming benefit. Using fantasies of positive patterns as a way of practicing them.

16. Courage. Reducing any unrealistic fears and aversions one is held back by. Not letting fears get in the way of doing what is best.

There are several subcategories under each of these skill groups. Appendix 1 presents the Psychological Skills Axis, a list of 62 psychological skills that forms a more complete list of what people need to learn to do for optimum functioning. The sixteen categories above are the names of the groups in that listing, but they cover fairly well the requirements for mental health.

Why were these skills chosen?

Productivity: The most fundamental characteristic separating living things from inanimate beings is goal-oriented activity: trying to do something, expending effort. With enough effort, it is possible to cultivate any of the other skills, but lack of productivity keeps people stuck.

Joyousness: Two major engines driving productivity are the quest for positive reinforcement and the avoidance of pain. Without the ability to feel good about reinforcing events, the motivation engine falters. Joyousness, feeling good, is also defensible as an end in itself, because it is by definition central to happiness.

Kindness: Toward what should we direct our efforts and productivity? Our own health and survival is an obvious choice; this is called self-care. But to really elevate the quality of existence, we work as well toward the welfare and happiness of others; kindness is the basis of ethics.

Honesty: In interacting with others and with oneself, people communicate. Without being able to depend upon the truth of communications, commerce, family relations, and other interpersonal dealings break down: we need honesty for communication to work.

Fortitude: In dealing with the world, just as it's good to feel joyous over good things, it's good to have regulated emotion when unwanted things happen: to feel enough negative emotion to assist in dealing with unwanted events, but not overwhelming negative emotion that interferes with coping. The ability to come up with reasonable responses to hardship is fortitude.

Good decisions: People have evolved the capacity to react to situations not just by instinct, but by careful decision-making, and this is a very important psychological skill. When people make decisions together, we can call this joint decision-making; in the subset of joint decisions where they start with opposing interests, we call this conflict-resolution.

Respectful talk and nonviolence: These are two very important extensions of the principle of kindness. They each deserve a special title all their own in the list of important psychological skills and ethical principles.

Friendship-building: People are social animals, and cultivating positive relationships is necessary for meaningful life as well as an assistance to survival and preservation of the species. Happiness appears to be proportional to the quality of relationships.

Self-discipline: The best decisions do not always coincide with what feels best at the moment. Acting so as to accomplish a goal, even at the expense of immediate pleasure, is self-discipline.

Loyalty: This is a complement to friendship-building: it's the ability to preserve relationships and to honor commitments. Loyalty does not mean giving unfair advantages to one's cronies or family members, and part of the skill of loyalty is deciding when not to do things for your fellow tribe-members.

Conservation: This skill is practiced at the individual level by being thrifty and nonwasteful, saving rather than spending, applying self-discipline to finances and possessions and one's use of time. Conservation on the global level is humanity saving rather than recklessly using up the resources of the earth. Especially in this age, conservation must be a prominent part of a code of ethics.

Self-care: A very large fraction of physical and mental health problems could be avoided if people enacted what we know about what is healthy and safe to do. The single habit of avoiding "recreational" drugs (including alcohol, cannabis, and nicotine) could make a huge difference to society. Care regarding diet, exercise, sleep, driving, head trauma, noise exposure, sun exposure, and risky behaviors can accomplish wonders for health and safety. I list being careful about other people's health and safety in this category, because people's fates are so closely intertwined.

Compliance: If human beings are to avoid violence to settle disputes, the "rule of law" is the best alternative to the "law of club and fang." The skill of compliance means contributing to fostering the rule of law by obeying those rules and laws and edicts from authority which are reasonable and just. Compliance does not mean surrendering one's ethical sense to an authority, and deciding when not to obey is part of this skill.

Positive fantasy rehearsal: In order to foster all the skills mentioned so far, a potent tool is to practice those skills in imagination, and to avoid practicing their opposites – this is positive fantasy rehearsal. Current society supplies models and practice opportunities for cruelty and violence through entertainment media, including videogames, in huge quantities. If the time and energy spent in fantasy practice of being a "shooter" could be applied to positive fantasy rehearsal of psychological skills, the world would be vastly improved. Ways of accomplishing this are a major topic of this book.

Courage: In carrying out the best decisions, we will often run up against fears and aversions that tell us to avoid something that our best judgment tells us to face; at this point courage is necessary to help us take the right course.

What do these skills have to do with mental health? My choices about what to include on the psychological skills axis resulted from spending a few years asking myself, regarding each person who presented to me for psychological treatment, and each person I read about with mental health problems, "What could this person learn to do that would make these problems better?" Kids with "conduct disorders" almost all needed more skills of kindness, honesty, nonviolence, respectful talk, friendship-building, and good decision-making. People with depression almost all need more ability to celebrate their own good acts, the good acts of others, and the blessings of fate – joyousness skills. Many depressed people have somehow gotten into habits of overreacting with demoralization to the frustrations of life; they can benefit from enhanced fortitude skills. A large part of mental distress seems to spring from conflicts and hostility between people; the skills of joint decision making, respectful talk, nonviolence, and friendship-building can relieve much of this. People with attention problems usually can greatly benefit from increased productivity and self-discipline skills. Anxiety problems by definition are lessened by increased courage skills, and relaxation skills (a subskill of self-care); those with social anxiety usually benefit greatly from studying the art of friendship-building, as well as developing courage skills. A large fraction of lifestyle related medical problems could be alleviated by heightened self-care skills; self-care as applied to not starting drugs of abuse would in itself eliminate huge amounts of psychopathology. Many mental health problems are connected with poverty; these have the potential to be vastly reduced with enough productivity, conservation and thrift, good decisions, and kindness – *not* just by people in poverty, but by the whole society. Some of the "good decisions" include those by governments, regarding how to harness the labor of people in ways that are good for humanity and also pay a living wage. The vast mental health toll exacted by violent crime and warfare and the threat of violence could be alleviated given enough good decision-making (including joint decisions or conflict-resolution), kindness, friendship-building, respectful talk, and of course, nonviolence.

Having made my career in the mental health field, I feel confident in saying that training of psychological skills is perhaps the most broadly successful strategy in the long-term relief and prevention of psychiatric symptoms. Under the terms behavior therapy and cognitive-behavior-therapy fall many types of skill-training interventions that have

21

proved successful for depression, anxiety, drug and alcohol abuse, impulsivity, aggression, marital discord, and many other sorts of psychological problems. The skills of revising thoughts and behaviors and emotional responses that people acquire by cognitive behavior therapy are imparted by an educational process. There is no reason why those skills can not be taught in purely educational, settings, and several pieces of research verify that this is the case. For example, simply reading and using David Burns's book *Feeling Good*, which is an explication of cognitive therapy principles in dealing with depression, has been found to have a positive effect with depressed individuals. What if universal education included the learnings that have allowed people to overcome depression, anxiety, impulsivity, violence, and so forth? Could we prevent a vast fraction of the mental health problems of humanity before they begin?

Some might argue, "There is no reason to burden the schools with the sorts of learnings that only a very few psychologically disturbed individuals ever need." The obvious rebuttal is that psychological symptoms and maladaptive habits are the rule, not the exception, with human beings. About 30% of US youth in grades 6 to 10 are involved in bullying, with about 13% as bullies, 11% as victims, and 6% as both. Over two million Americans are incarcerated, as of this writing. The National Comorbidity Survey Replication found lifetime prevalences of psychiatric disorders as follows: anxiety disorders, 29%; mood disorders (including depression) 21%; impulse-control disorders, 25%; substance use disorders, 15%, and any disorder, 46%. Thus a little under half the US. population in this survey met criteria for one of these disorders some time during life. My strong guess is that almost all of the other 54% could benefit greatly from improvement in some psychological skills.

Psychological skills in the service of better life

Even in a world which we can only imagine, in which there are no psychiatric or behavioral disorders, it would still be important to teach psychological skills, for the sake of making life better. For the sake of making more satisfying relationships, more focused and effective work, more joyous experience of existence, more kindness among people, it would be worthwhile to invest lots of time in the study of these skills. Psychological skills are not just for the relief of disorders, but for better life.

Skills are synergistic

Isn't it a little ambitious to take on teaching the whole set of psychological skills? Why not just problem-solving and decision-making – if people consistently make good decisions, we've done well enough. Why not just kindness – the elimination of cruelty and promotion of kind behavior is certainly a formidable enough task to take on by itself. Why not just self-discipline – surely this is a major key to success in any endeavor. What about just taking on a subset of self-care, the prevention of drug abuse – that in itself is enough to improve society dramatically.

The reason to teach the entire range of psychological skills is that they facilitate one another. Their development is synergistic.

For example: People so lacking in joyousness and self-reinforcement skills that they wind up depressed are likely to suffer impairment in productivity, self-discipline, fortitude, and several other skills. Some people with very low self-discipline tend to do selfish things in the pursuit of immediate pleasure, and thus spoil relationships. People poor at friendship-building tend to suffer from loneliness that impairs productivity; their lack of social support when bad things happen may lower their fortitude. Those with huge fears of failure tend to avoid attempting new skills and practicing at them, for fear of imperfect performance. This avoidance of practice greatly impairs productivity.

Let's imagine more examples of synergy, this time in the positive direction. Those who exercise often for the sake of self-care tend to improve their mood, and make

24

joyousness more possible. Those good at conservation in the sense of saving money tend to have a backlog of financial resources that can be used in case of adversity, and thus fortitude is easier. Those good at conflict-resolution tend to keep friends and be more loyal; they thus have much more energy to put into productivity because of not having to spend so much of it on interpersonal conflict. Honest people tend to be more compliant with the law and kinder, because they are more hesitant to lie their way out of exploiting others. Those who can use self-reinforcement (a subskill under joyousness) are likely to be much more successful at delay of gratification or self-discipline, because they are able to supply some pleasure to themselves to compensate for the pleasure they have forsworn.

My conclusion is that even if schools wish to promote only one psychological skill, they will probably have more success if they attempt to teach all of them!

Who is responsible for imparting skills?

Where should psychological skills be taught? Are psychological skills the bailiwick of parents, religious institutions, scouting organizations, the mental health system, or should they be taught in schools? Perhaps one of the reasons why the state of psychological skill development in society at large is not higher is that it is a job that is not reliably carried out anywhere.

The advantages of schools are several. First, the enterprise really is educational, and the same methods that are most successful in teaching other skills should work with psychological skills. Second, like other educational endeavors, "time on task" is crucial. School is one of the places where children spend large amounts of time. By contrast, in the health care system, once a week sessions for any substantial length of time go only to a small fraction of children; daily sessions (which are optimum for education) are nearly unheard of. And third, as I will discuss at more length soon, it is possible for the learning of psychological skills to be linked with the learning of reading and writing and other academic skills, so that more than one mission is being accomplished at once. Fourth, the teaching of psychological health skills in schools would, if successful, destigmatize these skills. Despite progress, there are still far too many people who feel that working on anger control or relaxation training or practicing "not getting down on yourself" or "celebrating your own choices" are something that only a scary group of people called the mentally ill should have to do.

Positive emotional climate

Despite the above considerations, and despite the title of this book, I am ambivalent about recommending that all schools take on the teaching of psychological skills! It is a delicate job, and harm can be done by botching it. To create in children an attitude of cynicism, revulsion, or derision toward the learning of psychological skills is a harmful outcome that far outweighs that of creating negative attitudes toward less important subjects. The large fraction of my child and adolescent patients who have told me, "I hate math," gives a warning about how schools often fail dramatically in the most important task of education: to increase the learner's appetite for more education. The teaching of psychological skills, like the teaching of mathematics or history or science, requires a great deal of careful planning and thought. But for psychological skills, even more than for most other subjects, a positive emotional climate is crucial. I have walked the halls of some schools while hearing frequent loud, angry screaming, originating primarily from teachers. These are schools where teaching the "tones of approval" exercise or the art of staying "cool and calculating" in the face of frustration would provoke only cynicism and mockery from the students. In addition, a psychological skills curriculum should not be imposed upon a teacher; the teacher who feels that the curriculum in question is "psychobabble" will not be an effective teacher. (To be fair: depending upon the curriculum, such a teacher might be correct.)

One of the reasons I have written this book is so that school personnel can "try on" images of teaching psychological skills in their imaginations. If the images I describe stir up positive excitement, there's a chance that they can be transcribed into reality. If they provoke derision or a long string of reasons why the methods would never work, they probably will not work.

The time crunch

The most common objection I've heard to teaching psychological skills in schools is that there is no time. With pressure to meet goals for academic subjects, many school personnel feel that there is not a minute left over to devote to another subject. This objection is sometimes raised even in special education classes and schools specifically for children with serious emotional disorders!

But this problem, I believe, has two solutions: first is the interweaving of psychological skills subject matter with practice in reading and writing. That is: when a student learns to read, the reading has to be about something! Why not let that something be psychological skills? I have written stories and instruction on psychological skills, designed for the most beginning readers up to rather advanced readers. When a student practices writing, the writing too has to be about something. Why not practice writing stories that model psychological skills, essays on the process whereby someone made a decision, sample dialogues of good conflict resolution, sample dialogues of positive social conversation, and many other psychological skill-exercising topics?

The second solution is interweaving of interpersonal skills training with training in techniques of individual tutoring. What are the characteristics of a good individual tutor? The good tutor is a good listener to the student; an empathic observer of the student's emotional state; a maintainer of an upbeat, cheerful attitude even in the face of some frustration; a good balancer of the use of authority with the use of persuasion and conciliation; a builder of morale; an enthusiastic and effective giver of positive reinforcement; a careful calculator of whether to move to a harder or easier task or stay at the current level; a modeler of joyous and goal-oriented work; a planner who comes to the encounter prepared; a careful decider on the proper mix of nurturing and toughness; a dependable appointment-keeper. These requirements for the ideal tutor have very high overlap with the interpersonal characteristics of the ideal boss, employee, spouse, friend, or parent. Thus: training older children in the art of tutoring younger children (or peers) is a great way of teaching universally useful interpersonal skills. But at the same time, such training also provides us with a cadre of workers who can provide one-on-one tutoring in academic skills, thus fostering our academic mission as well. And a good deal of research concludes that one-on-one tutoring is much more effective than group instruction.

Conservative or liberal?

Some social and emotional learning programs have been criticized on political grounds. Leaders of one or another political tribe have seen programs as indoctrination into the views of the other tribe.

The psychological skills axis was constructed without a particular political viewpoint in mind, but rather in a quest for the skills that tend to produce happiness in oneself and others. There is great room for disagreement on how to apply them, including which skill should predominate when they are in conflict. For example: does the principle of self-care dictate not only absolute abstinence from alcohol, but strong protest of others' use of it, or do joyousness and friendship-building point toward less rigidity? Does the principle of conservation, of non-waste, mean that a certain construction project should be abandoned, or does it mean that undue time and money should not be wasted on barriers to it? Does the principle of kindness mean that government should require employers to provide certain benefits to employees, or does the principle of permitting freedom, of non-bossiness, (subsumed under joint decision-making) mean that the employers and employees should be able to make their own decisions? There is plenty of room, within the psychological skills framework, for differing political opinions.

But the skills themselves appear to have validity that transcend partisan divisions. Which political group would like to go on record that productivity is not good, that people should not feel good, that people should not be kind to each other, that honesty is not necessary, that decision-making should be haphazard and arbitrary, that violence is preferable to peace, and that people should not have friends?

All of society has a stake in the nurturing of mentally healthy, ethical individuals. I would hope that we can pursue that goal without any political group fearing the loss of votes. But there will probably always be certain political groups that do feel that they will lose votes by the nurturing of psychological skills, and perhaps those groups deserve to lose some votes.

So far, however, the idea that psychological skill teaching has major effects on the choices made in society is aspirational. It is more a "vision" than current large-scale reality. On a smaller scale, however, results have often been very positive.

Will artificial intelligence take over the job?

At this time, predictions are being made (more by "tech" type folks than by "education" types, it appears to me) that artificial intelligence is poised to do better at tutoring and teaching than human beings can do.

As Yogi Berra is reported to have said, "The hardest thing to predict is the future." If artificial intelligence produces a generation of competent, engaged, joyful learners, that will be great. However, I'm not holding my breath for that to take place.

I was a school child when another wondrous technological innovation promised to revolutionize education: television. I took a Spanish class offered to all children in the district, through the miracle of this innovation. But television also delivered millions of models of violent behavior and provided huge distraction from more productive pursuits. Then came the personal computer technology, and with it the ready implementation of B.F. Skinner's programmed instruction through "teaching machines": providing a bit of instruction, asking the learner to demonstrate understanding, and giving feedback. Theoretically, learners can go at their own rate, with an infinitely patient teacher. But somehow the vision of students happily sitting in front of screens, learning with computer optimized methods, forming a cohort of very literate critical thinkers, hasn't come to pass. And computer chips have ushered in an era in which millions of children (particularly males) spend most of their discretionary time in virtual rehearsal of violent acts, in the form of video games, while reading of books is neglected.

What if it's true that education takes place best in the context of a positive relationship? What if learning is fostered by positive social interactions? What if imaginary people on screens, or even androids or robots, somehow don't fulfill our need for human connection?

When I homeschooled with my daughters, I spent many hours sitting beside them on a couch or at a table, reading books together, working problems together, talking about what we were learning. These were some of the happiest hours of my life. They were also good for my psyche, in that I got to practice patience, kindness, good decision-making, joyousness, and other important psychological skills. I got to remind myself, or learn for the first time, about many of the most important ideas humanity has come up with.

Thus this book emphasizes positive interactions between human beings rather than apps and artificial intelligence. If it turns out that the next wave of technology creates a better world through much more effective education, I'll be very happy to admit having been wrong!

Chapter 2: Components of the Vision

What isn't enough

Here's what is not enough, and can even be harmful: a psychological skills or social and emotional learning curriculum, isolated from the rest of the school's operations – a set of lesson plans given to a teacher, sometimes with a mandate of "You must teach this."

What else we need

The vision described here is not just a course, but a way of creating a school environment. In other words, the fostering of psychological skills does not just take place during a certain segment of allocated time – it is part of every course, throughout the school day, everything that goes on at school. It involves a very concerted effort toward creating a "positive emotional climate": setting things up so that people like, help, approve of, and enjoy each other. It has as one of the major goals that learners can self-educate: that they can use educational materials (including that most venerated, avoided, and maligned one, the book) to learn on their own. It also seeks to create ways in which people can meaningfully and joyously connect with one another around the tasks of learning.

Here are some components.

1. Focus on the goals and skills.

There is frequent reference to the goals (happiness of self and others) and skills (productivity, joyousness, kindness, ...) and celebration of positive models of them, not just by the SEL (Social and Emotional Learning) teacher, not just during SEL class, but throughout the school day, by all school personnel. Psychological skills learning is integrated with art, music, reading, writing, math, and all other school subjects!

2. Resistant, compliant, and goal-directed.

What is a person's stance toward learning, working, or doing any other activity? In the resistant stance, the person is in an active adversarial relationship with whoever is trying to get them to do the activity or task. Sometimes resistance is through defiance, and sometimes it is through deception. The two forces are in a competitive contest with one another.

In the compliant stance, the person has decided that their needs are best met by going along with the directives of the other person. They follow the rules, but there's no motivation to do any more than is asked of them.

In the goal-directed stance, the person wants to accomplish something, whether or not someone else tells them to. They do things on their own to accomplish those goals, and they see teachers or coaches as collaborators who offer input that may be helpful in reaching their goals.

Part of the job of educators is not just to observe these stances in their students, but to help move them along the continuum toward goal-directedness (provided that the goals are good ones). Part of the way this job is accomplished is to talk about it and think about it. This includes enlisting students in self-monitoring, generating ideas about it, and making it a central focus of education.

If education takes this seriously, it has to acknowledge that what might be a good goal for one learner may not be a good one for another. Not all students have to excel at literary criticism, just as not all have to excel at repair of heating and ventilation systems.

3. The magic of one-to-one

Hopefully we can depart in a very major way from the model where the students are expected to sit in a large group and listen to the teacher, speak one at a time, or do seat work. We move, for a large portion of the day, to the model where a learner does individualized work with a well-trained tutor.

Where can the person-power for one-to-one tutoring be obtained? From older peers taught to tutor younger peers. This benefits both tutors and their students.

4. Hierarchy-ology, challenge level

One of the benefits of one-to-one instruction is that a fundamental tenet of education can be realized: the challenges for the particular learner are arranged to be not too hard, not too easy, but in the zone of optimal challenge. Tutors and teachers are trained to find the right point on the "hierarchy of difficulty" for each learner. But also, part of the culture is that learners are trained to contribute to finding their zones of optimal challenge and communicating about them – to feel no shame in saying, "I need to move down the hierarchy of difficulty for a while, and work my way back up," or to not be judged as conceited when they communicate, "I think I'm ready to move up the hierarchy from this."

5. Tutor training for peers

Teaching students to be tutors for other students is a central activity of the school. As mentioned before, the psychological skills involved in being a good tutor – kindness, ability to listen, ability to find the learner's ideal degree of challenge, balancing authority with giving freedom, concentration and focus, joyous attitude toward work, ability to follow directions, and others – are the same skills useful in being a good work supervisor, employee, romantic partner or spouse, friend, or family member. Thus training students to tutor other students is not just an attempt to exploit their free labor, but a means toward their own psychological growth.

6. Mental health for teachers.

The workday of a teacher should not be conducive to burnout, but should contain lots of payoff: seeing students make progress and seeing the efforts toward a positive emotional climate bear fruit. The workday should include adequate down time, adequate exercise, adequate and adequate non-stressful interaction with others. Not least, teachers, like students, should have the ability to take a bathroom break whenever needed. The career of teacher should be greatly respected by society. Verbal or physical abuse of teachers by students should be prevented to the fullest extent possible. This would be a desired outcome of successful psychoeducation beginning in the earliest years. Where psychoeducation has not been successful enough, teachers (as well as other students) need to be protected from abuse by students, if necessary by removal of the student from the classroom. Education for parents on rules of verbal interaction with teachers may be necessary in preserving teachers' mental health.

7. Giving to and receiving from parents.

The goals of parenting and schooling are the same: to foster the development of people with the skills to be happy, to help others be happy, and to be resilient. Insofar as possible, parents and educators work together toward those goals. Parents can be helped to work with their own children on schoolwork, to help other children at school, and to create a mental-health friendly environment at home. In turn, those parents with the time and energy to do so can contribute much to the school's mission. The school could come close to guaranteeing that no parent should feel lonely or alone. It could be a place where parents can connect with other parents. The tutoring curricula that are central to the school should help parents to have positive interactions with their own children, with other people's children, with other parents, and with their spouses – it is not unrealistic to include these goals as part of the school's mission, for however large or small a subset of parents is available to take part.

8. Enlisting other helpers.

Student teachers, community volunteers, and others, as well as parents, can be trained and monitored. There are large obstacles to the recruitment of the person-power that education desperately needs: fear of sexual, physical, and verbal abuse of children, violence, miseducation, indoctrination into maladaptive philosophies, and lawsuits and negative publicity resulting from those. In other words, the psychological skill deficiencies that are rampant in society are a large impediment to gathering a labor force to remedy those deficiencies in the next generation. Investment of much time in training, during which time the trainer can thoroughly get to know the prospective helper, before the helper is ever entrusted with work with a student, is one option for solving this dilemma.

9. Ditching the guild mentality.

Despite the need for careful screening of helpers in psychoeducation, we should abandon the idea that only certified teachers can or should teach. Instead, the school can be a place where enlisting people to teach, training them to teach well, and monitoring to see how well they are teaching, goes on constantly. By such a model, we upgrade the role of teachers: they don't just teach; they also teach others to teach and to self-educate, and they monitor the quality of all the education that goes on.

10. Directly useful work.

Building maintenance and repair, care of the grounds, cleaning, clerical tasks, information technology, food preparation, and food growing – in most schools these tasks are done by people whom the students don't know, don't interact with, and don't learn from. But each useful thing that a student learns how to do enriches that student's life. Plus, many of the tasks provide a contribution to mental health: a break from "sit down, be quiet, listen to directions" regimen. Insofar as possible, the workers who do these tasks at school can show and teach students how to do them, with the assistance of other teaching personnel. Useful work procedures are video recorded, and students create written and spoken directions for how to carry out the procedure. These in turn become part of the curriculum for the school.

11. "Life of the mind."

The phrase, "life of the mind," has come to mean taking joy in discovery, joy in understanding the big ideas that human culture has come up with, the wondrous creations of classical writings, the pleasure of intellectual discussion.

The philosophy is that there is time in the educational days for both: for how to fix a dripping faucet, and for whether or not there is free will; for cooking, and for research methodology; for helping move furniture, and for the nature of utilitarian ethics; for repairing machines and solving equations. A task is to pick the challenges for each learner that are not too hard, not too easy, but just right.

People differ in their dispositions toward working with physical objects versus ideas. In the envisioned school, there is an attempt to make both sorts of work as fun and gratifying as possible, but not to make a Procrustean bed where all students must complete the same courses in order to graduate.

12. Physical exercise.

One of the best antidotes to both restlessness and lethargy, as well as a direct contributor to mental health, is lots of physical exercise. We discuss ways of promoting this later on.

13. Cooperative orientation.

Competition can be a motivating and fun element of life – especially when not "cutthroat." But the more the school culture can include activities where each participant is not only doing the best they can, but also wishing for their comrades to do as well as they can, the more the culture corrects an overemphasis on the competitive, adversarial mentality. A future chapter will go into more detail on cooperative activities, including the "cooperative debate."

14. Diversity of activities

There's enough time in the school day for exercise of self-discipline, friendship-building, joyousness – activities are not mutually exclusive. Repetitive drill and practice is an extremely useful part of learning to do anything better, and it should not be eliminated from education. In fact, a major goal should be to gradually increase students' tolerances and even enjoyment of mental endurance, just as people gradually get into better physical shape. But many other activities should balance out drill and practice. Learning through projects, discussion, reading, public speaking, field observations – there's time in the day for all of it. No method of learning should be rejected out of hand.

15. Testing and monitoring, used and not misused.

Anti-testing sentiment often springs from seeing tests misused in various ways: to evaluate teachers based on the outcomes, to orient the entire educational enterprise to teaching to the test, to crowd out non-test-related activities in a spirit of dread of negative test results, to judge and even close schools with poor test results. Testing is misused when significant fractions of the testees miss very large fractions of the test questions, and find the tests frustrating and aversive. It's misused when teachers face negative consequences for low scores that have nothing to do with the quality of their teaching. It's misused when test prep displaces the pursuit of more important goals.

But frequent testing and monitoring of outcomes can be used totally differently: to help the students recognize their own progress and celebrate it; to help the tutors and teachers see if they are on the right track, and to adjust or stay on course accordingly. Importantly, judicious

41

testing can help tutors and teachers in the vital task of deciding what is too hard, too easy, and just right for a given child. The mastery learning paradigm, to be discussed later, depends upon measurement and assessment of mastery. One key is comparing test results to the student's previous results, and to the desired goals. Comparison to the performances of other students has its place, but should be done when consciously chosen rather than by default. Usually the best comparisons are with nameless large norming samples from which percentiles can be derived.

Testing should not treat children as if they are interchangeable parts of a machine. The best tests arrange items in order of difficulty and allow either the tester or a computer program to land on the region where the items are at the zone of optimal challenge for the individual. When the items get too hard, there's no reason to give harder ones; when they are easy enough, there's no reason to give easier ones. The test provides not just an outcome measure but a guide to figuring out the zone of optimal challenge for instruction.

16. Emotional climate, interpersonal environment.

How much do people agree or disagree with the following, regarding the school they attend, teach at, or help administer?
1. School is a place where people are mad at one another.
2. At this school, people are kind to one another.

3. At this school, people study how to get along and communicate well, and they use those learnings in the school itself, daily.
4. Of the things that teachers and students say to each other, many more of the utterances communicate approval than disapproval.

I fear that in many schools, people would strongly agree with the first and strongly disagree with the others. Much has been written on what sorts of communications tend to promote harmony in human relations. (These writings include my first book, *Talking It Out*, everything written by Marshall Rosenberg, and many other works.) In the envisioned schools, students, tutors, teachers, and all other personnel study how to express observations, needs, feelings, and requests in good ways and observe the effects of using these principles at school.

Why is emotional climate important? A large amount of research has demonstrated that emotional climates are intimately related to mental health. Even for the conditions that clearly have a strong biological component, such as bipolar disorder and schizophrenia, emotional climates play a strong role in how well people do.

How should we measure the emotional climate? Anonymous surveys are important in assessing the climate of a group. When a sufficiently trusting environment has been achieved (in other words, when there is already enough of a positive emotional climate) students should be able to openly discuss the emotional climates they are living in.

17. Purposeful and preserved writing.

Here's a vision: writings in schools are often for the purpose of helping other people rather than just being judged. Writing assignments in schools are often, perhaps usually, read by the teacher only, assigned a grade, and afterwards discarded or forgotten. But the best purpose of writing is to preserve things worth saying, so that they may help others. (Shakespeare confidently included in one of his sonnets, "So long as men can breathe, and eyes can see, so long lives this….") The vision is that the thrills of creating something of lasting benefit will be harnessed in writing exercises. Students can encode in their writing positive models of psychological skills, conflict-resolution conversations, social conversations, 12 thought exercises, decision processes, reflections exercises, lists of choice points, lists of options for choice points, lists of pros and cons for options, lists of conflicts, provocations, and criticisms to practice with, instructions on how to tutor well, instructions on how to monitor tutoring, and others! These writings add to the bank of instructional materials for their own cohort, and for future cohorts of students.

18. Self-education.

Schooling can induce passivity. If there's no room for choice about the course, often you don't find out what that course will offer. You wait till the course starts before you start learning. You do the work that's assigned to you, and no more. When the course ends, you do nothing more to preserve or continue your learnings.

The contrasting philosophy is to purposefully nurture, monitor, and celebrate each learner's growth toward competence in self-education. A major goal for every learner is to acquire the ability to: get curious about something or generate a wish for some skills, figure out how to get the necessary instructional materials, do the work independently or recruit others to join, and learn, without any formal structure imposed.

In other words, a major goal of formal educational institutions is to make themselves unnecessary! Or at least, to figure out how to foster self-education that can thrive alongside the additional value-added components schools supply.

19. Critical thinking about media.

The "media diet" or "information diet" of most children, adolescents, and young adults in this era, at least in the USA, comes more from electronic entertainment or social media than from educational media, including books. It doesn't do to depend upon a "Thou shalt not kill" poster when young people are spending hundreds or even thousands of hours on Grand Theft Auto, Call of Duty, or whatever violent entertainments have become hits in the era in which you're reading this. It doesn't do to depend upon the approval teachers give for prosocial productions when the student gets many more "likes" on social media for mean-spirited productions. It doesn't work to depend upon assigned readings in science while their "feeds" are providing patently false information. Helping students to exercise wise and ethical judgment about how they want to feed their minds has to be a central goal of education. This goal is especially difficult in an era in which mistrust of science, intellectualism, and scholarship is rampant. (I read recently about a course of action advocated by a large number of Nobel Prize laureates; someone responded that people in the USA are sick and tired of elites telling them what to do.) Since most of our knowledge comes not from our direct observation, but from the observations of others, figuring out whom to trust is not a simple task.

20. Schools for learning versus sorting.

Should all students have to pass certain courses, and an exit exam, to get a diploma (e.g. for high school)? If not, some people argue, then the diploma doesn't "mean anything." The worry is that employers and the next level of educators will not be able to use the grades and the diplomas as a way of selecting whom to hire or admit to their institutions. The assignment of grades and the awarding, versus non-awarding, of diplomas, according to this practice, sort people into various categories of competence and quality.

A problem with such sorting is that even though the world has a huge variety of roles that people can play, the current sorting methods tend to evaluate people approximately as if every student were aspiring to become a college professor. Many of those who are destined to carry out truly essential tasks for humanity – laying and repairing our water pipes, growing our food, building and repairing our housing, moving our things from one place to another… – often get repeated clear messages from schooling that "You are not as good as those others." The result is too often a hostility toward schooling, learning, science, the "elites" who everyone thinks are so smart, and sadly, hostility toward the self, building up over years.

A related problem is that students quickly discern that high grades mean "You did better than most of the students sitting around you," and low grades mean the opposite. Thus, each student is thrust into competition with the students who happen to be in the same school and the same course. (I have wondered if this explains part of the popularity of the *Hunger Games* novels and movies: is forced mortal combat among adolescents a metaphor for the unwelcome competition fostered in schools?)

Let's ponder what may seem a radical idea: it is not a major job of schools to facilitate the choices of subsequent schools or employers on whom to accept and reject. Those institutions can do their own work on selection! This is particularly true when the sorting function comes into conflict with the goal of helping the learner gain the skills most useful for that learner's life. For example, a grading and ranking and diploma-granting system should not promote the thought pattern of, "I've already been sorted into the group that won't succeed, so why should I waste futile efforts trying to prove myself to be a scholar?"

On the other hand: there are advantages to schools' providing credentials to learners. Obtaining proof and documentation of one's competence can be motivating for the learner as well as useful for the society that needs those competences. Allowing students to win, or not win, teachers' endorsements as competent in various areas of expertise is a rational alternative to "all have won and all must have prizes." But the best system gives the opportunity for every student to be successful – at some things worth succeeding at, not necessarily at a one-size-fits-all set of standards. For some students, certification as competent in dishwashing, loading and unloading moving vans, tilling soil, harvesting crops, operating a backhoe, and being dependable, careful, and respectful while doing so, may be wonderful goals of education, just as certification in various levels of calculus, writing, chemistry, and others may also be great goals, and sometimes for the same students. What does not make sense is to set up an all or none where all students must be either be scholars in traditional academic subjects or become one of the non-chosen ones who are deemed, and who deem themselves, inferior.

21. The mastery learning paradigm.

Traditional education holds constant the time allocated to a given course, and measures the degree of mastery of course material; such a measure is to be reflected in the course grade. In the mastery learning paradigm, the goal is a certain degree of mastery, and what is allowed to vary is the amount of time taken to achieve it. Measurement of the degree of mastery is done repeatedly to monitor progress toward the goal. Such measurement also informs teacher and learner as to whether the current methods are on track to produce mastery, or whether other methods should be tried. Obviously, the mastery learning paradigm is more applicable with individualized instruction than with group instruction.

The philosophy is not, "Mastery learning is good; traditional courses and grades are bad." But the mastery learning paradigm is held in mind as a major alternative to be used when practical.

22. Decision-making.

Central to mental health is making good decisions. How do we do that? The art and science of decision making should be a central part of educational curricula. Research has demonstrated the value for mental health of certain subskills of decision making, such as generating options and generating pros and cons for options. Thorough study of the components of careful decisions, case studies of good and bad decisions, much practice in components such as generating options and pros and cons, and examination of the quality of one's own decisions are part of the core curriculum,

23. Fiction as a training ground

People spend a great fraction of their lives in fictitious worlds: the worlds created by TV shows, lyrics of songs, videogames, movies, novels, their own daydreams, and others.

Fiction can provide practice in all sorts of mental maneuvers, among them: 1) Taking the perspective of a character, recognizing the emotions, motives, and

49

unspoken thoughts of a character. 2) Finding good and bad examples of psychological skills. (The good examples are usually harder to find!) 3) For good decisions and bad decisions characters made, analyzing what, in the decision process, went right or wrong. 4) Analyzing the consequences of decisions – what happened as a result of what the character decided? Would that consequence be likely to happen in real life? 5) When a character made a bad decision, what would have been a better one, and why? 6) What is the nature of the relationships between the characters? How can we describe relationships in general, and apply our descriptors to the ones in the story? 7) What part of the psyche of the audience is being appealed to, to attract the audience? Is the author appealing to the "higher" or "lower" pleasures? 8) Practicing generating fictitious situations to practice with, and fictitious positive responses to them, that are worth rehearsing.

There's a great deal of evidence that "fantasy rehearsal," practicing patterns in imagination, can be a major aid to learning, for better or for worse. Fiction can lead to either positive or negative fantasy rehearsal, and the best schools will harness fiction maximally for rehearsal of positive patterns of thought, behavior, and emotion.

24. Health education, including pharmacology.

Drug abuse accounts for a very significant fraction of psychopathology. According to my experience, if you ask the average teenager who takes up using a certain drug to list the adverse effects of that drug, you will get an answer deserving a failing grade. Few can explain the basic neuronal processes whereby addiction gets entrenched. Few understand the following principle: a drug that directly stimulates pleasure centers in the brain undermines the motivation to seek pleasure in more effortful ways, such as relationships and accomplishments. Although some argue that drug abuse is impervious to rational weighings of pros and cons, such rational thought is one of the central activities of drug treatments that have worked, including motivational interviewing. Rational thought should work lots better as a preventive than as a cure.

Similarly, although many people with anorexia nervosa are very good students, very few of them are experts on the adverse effects of under-nutrition on the skin, the bones, the brain, and other organs.

A large fraction of adolescents appear to be attempting to function in a condition of sleep deprivation, often because the clocks in their brains are set to the pattern of going to sleep late and getting up late. Very few of them understand the nature of sleep rhythms or are able to list the experiences that reset those rhythms. (Bright light, exercise, eating, and being out of bed in the morning set the clock earlier; the same things at night set them later.)

25. Peace and conflict-resolution studies

How can human beings learn to get along with each other, without hurting each other? This is a subject about which many smart people have written and thought, but which is neglected in typical school curricula. But ignorance of this topic directly threatens the continued existence of the human species, in addition to causing great unhappiness in families. Conflict-resolution, nonviolence, respectful talk, friendship-building, and kindness are psychological skills that bear directly upon this issue. The study of "nonviolence heroes," the history of nonviolent movements, case studies of successful mediation, alternatives to violence, and communication methods, should occupy a prominent place in school curricula.

Chapter 3: Ways to Teach Psychological Skills

Ten methods of influence

Teaching is a much more complex activity than just telling the learners what they need to know. In teaching *any* skills – academic, sports, psychological, or otherwise – there are ten methods of influence whereby one person can help another to learn, as follows.

1. Objective-formation, or goal-setting. The learner comes to *want* to improve in the skill.

2. Hierarchy: There is a series of small steps for the learner to progress along, with no one step being so large that it is a barrier to progress. The learner starts at a place on the hierarchy where he or she can experience lots of success. Whenever the degree of difficulty is too great or too little, the level quickly adjusts accordingly.

3. Relationship: The teacher has a positive relationship with the student; there is a positive emotional climate. The teacher is more effective if the student admires the teacher.

4. Attribution: People attribute to the learner the capacity to gain in the skill, rather than having a fixed and immutable degree of ability in it. The teacher creates positive visions for how life will be better with more of such skill.

5. Modeling: Many positive models of thought, feeling, and behavior patterns are available and observed. These include models stored in media and those presented in real life.

6. Practice: There's great opportunity for much practice of the skillful patterns, aiming toward fluent performance.

7. Reinforcement and punishment: There are incentives for positive performance, payoffs that motivate the learner. Positive reinforcement creates approach motivation; punishment creates avoidance motivation. Positive reinforcement tends to strengthen the relationship and model desirable behavior, whereas punishment can do the opposite.

8. Instruction: There are detailed explanations of how to perform skillfully.

9. Stimulus control: The environment elicits skillful patterns.

10. Monitoring: The learner's performance is repeatedly monitored. The teacher and learner get feedback, and they use it to improve the operation of the other 9 influences.

A mnemonic for these methods of influence is the words "Oh ram prism." These methods of influence, and specific ways of enacting them, will be discussed in chapters to follow. These methods of influence, together with the list of psychological skills, form what I have called the skills-by-methods-of-influence matrix. The intersections, where a certain method of influence is used to promote a certain skill, are ways of building skill.

Three major activities for psychoeducational sessions

Regarding the question, "How do we teach psychological skills," I've experimented with one-to-one psychological skills training sessions, consisting of three major activities. Each of these activities can be done in one-to-one sessions in school, or in classroom-wide or other group-wide activities.

1. Reading about psychological skills. The format I've come to appreciate the most uses writings programmed specifically for this purpose, where the chapters are divided into sections of about 150-300 words, and after each there is a question checking comprehension. In a social activity called *alternate reading*, two people take turns reading these sections aloud, while one of them answers the comprehension probes, and another provides feedback.

2. Psychological Skills Exercises. What do playing scales on a musical instrument, running to get in better shape, solving math problems, practicing dance steps, practicing foul shots in basketball, and composing essays have in common? They all are exercises to get more skilled at something. But for mental health skills, the use of structured, systematic exercises often gets short shrift.

How can psychological skills be exercised and practiced? One person talks while the other practices good listening techniques. People take turns thinking of options for the problems or choice points. People take turns thinking of celebrations, i.e. positive examples of psychological skills they have carried out. Students write dialogues illustrating good conflict-resolution or social conversation, or stories that model any psychological skills.

Just as reading practice can be combined with mental health education by reading books and handouts on mental health, writing practice can be combined with mental health by lots of written exercises. Some of that writing can add to the corpus of instruction for future cohorts of students.

I'll mention some psychological skills exercises in this book; the psychological skills curriculum that I've written includes two full length books on psychological skills exercises.

3. Social conversation. Part of each psychological skills session is unstructured social conversation. This activity tends to strengthen relationships between teachers and learners, foster increased verbal ability, enhance friendship-building skills, and serve various other ends.

The counterpart for group teaching is, of course, group discussions. Mental health, which overlaps almost completely with ethics, is in my opinion the most interesting topic that exists. The vision is that the invitation, "What are your questions or comments?" will be the signal for engaged, thoughtful, and fun discussions in which all learners participate.

Staff development

Staff for psychological skill training must, first of all, be carefully selected. And various training activities are in order before work with students starts. These are directed toward the goal that the various activities – reading, psychological skills exercises, social conversations, academic tutoring activities – can be conducted expertly. But much of the training of staff can be accomplished by teachers going through exactly the same training manuals that students use. These manuals describe the activities in great detail; the manuals deliver to both student and teacher the entire content of the curriculum. The model of teachers and students learning together is perhaps the most empowering and destigmatizing of all. My personal experience reinforces this idea: each time I conduct a psychological skills training session, I learn and practice. I often learn from the training materials, even when I wrote them – much of the most useful education consists in reminding ourselves of what we already know, and practicing it in another variation. Continual reading of psychological skills manuals and practice of psychological skills exercises has, I think, made me a happier, kinder, and more productive person; this should be one of the tests of any training program.

The ideal methods of psychological skill training for any given setting are still very much to be revised and refined. One of the chief methods of staff development should consist of teachers sharing with one another what important learnings they have come up with. These learnings, in turn, should be incorporated into revisions of written training materials.

Happy teachers

In order for psychological skills education to be carried out well, we need teachers who, at least, don't hate their jobs! Beyond that, we need environments conducive to real enjoyment and happiness of teachers. One of the major impediments to the happiness of teachers is violence, noncompliance, unkindness, and nonproductivity of students. When teachers are exhausted, irritable, and demoralized, their capacity to effectively teach and model psychological skills and to create a positive learning climate plummets. This in turn affects the psychological skills of students, in a vicious circle. The vicious circle can be turned to a virtuous circle: happier teachers can increase the psychological skills of students; this effect makes teaching more pleasant and rewarding.

The last thing I would like to see is teachers who are mandated to teach social and emotional learning, who would rather not, and who resent having to do so. The teaching of mental health should be a "coalition of the eager." Similarly undesirable is a rigid curriculum that permits no deviations, even if the teacher dislikes a certain portion of it. The teaching profession thrives when teachers are trusted to make good decisions, when they are given some autonomy. When they teach psychological skills in different ways, and when they have lots of time to communicate with one another about what works and what doesn't work, the conditions are ripe not only for faster progress in the accumulation of positive tactics, but also for happier teachers.

Students as tutors for other students

As mentioned before, one to one interaction is magical for education. "The best way to learn something is to teach it." When we enlist the aid of older students in teaching younger ones, both benefit. But tutors must be carefully selected, trained, and monitored in order for tutoring to be of most benefit to both students. With careful enough training, selection, and monitoring, students teaching other students can be a powerful, even revolutionary, force in education. More will be said about this later.

Chapter 3: Setting Psychological Skills Goals

A marketing department?

The first of the ten methods of influence was objective-formation, or goal-setting: creating the conditions under which children and adolescents come to *want* to get more psychologically skilled. You can lead a horse to water, but you can't make him drink; creating a "thirst" for knowledge and competence in the psychological skills is of high priority.

The most ubiquitous and inescapable method of getting people to want things in our society is advertising. So should we create advertisements for psychological skills, complete with pitches by whatever type of person is most persuasive to the target group? Should we post slogans on walls? Should we give pep talks to students, selling the desirability of psychological skills? Should we play and sing jingles? Should we engage students in creating their own advertisements, either in writing or in some other medium, thus taking advantage of the social psychological finding that attempting to persuade someone else of something, even in role-playing, tends to persuade the persuader? Should a school accumulate a growing bank of advertisements for psychological skills, with students voting on which are best, and with the best marketers honored for their creations?

My guess is that if the tools of the advertising and marketing trade were harnessed to convince children and adolescents of the value of psychological skills, they would be somewhat successful. Advertising is a very empirical science: if one method works better than another, that method gets chosen for the next round.

There's a certain amount of cynicism surrounding advertising, and rightly so, given how intrusive it is and how successfully it persuades people to part with their money in exchange for useless, cluttering, or even harmful things. There are ways of creating motivation other than advertising; let's think about some of them.

A more subtle method of motivation

There's a very different tactic available: helping the student to see the evidence the real world presents for the value of psychological skills, by thoroughly learning the vocabulary that names those skills.

The Sapir-Whorf hypothesis states that the words in a person's vocabulary and the syntax with which the person employs those words, do not just reflect the person's world view and competence in reacting to the world – they influence these, and to a great degree, determine them. Any specialized skill arena has its vocabulary: ballroom dancers speak of fifth position breaks, chess players speak of forks and pins, neurosurgeons speak of the third ventricle; lawyers speak of torts, statisticians speak of standard deviations and confidence intervals, and so forth. If someone were to try to become expert in any field without learning its specialized vocabulary, the road would be much more difficult, perhaps impossible.

There is a specialized vocabulary relevant to psychological skill development. The most fundamental words are those that name the psychological skills themselves: productivity, joyousness, kindness, honesty, fortitude, decision-making, conflict-resolution, nonviolence, and so forth. Another fundamental set is the words for emotions: awe, determination, compassion, lightheartedness, as well as the more familiar ones. Similarly, there are words for types of thoughts (listing options and choosing, celebrating your own choice…), types of verbal behaviors (commands and criticisms, reflections, follow-up questions, positive feedback) and many others.

Part of the goal of teaching the student these terms is that they become predisposed to see life as a series of opportunities to use particular psychological skills. For example: a student is assigned a lot of demanding homework. A student who is steeped in psychological skill terminology has the opportunity to think, "Here's a chance for me to use self-discipline and fortitude and productivity. As I do this, I want to use lots of "celebrating my own choices," so that I use my joyousness skills as well!" The student who is not accustomed to thinking in such terms might default to "What a bummer. That teacher is so bad for making me do this!"

When students get these terms thoroughly into their vocabularies, they are able to look at real life and to see for themselves the evidence for the value of the skills.

Accordingly, one of the major tasks carried out in the various programmed texts I have written is to give the student practice in seeing concrete examples of skills, thoughts, emotions, and behaviors, and to correctly classify them, using the terms they have been taught.

Also important is for the student to hear other people in their social environment using these words – that these words become "household phrases." If teachers and fellow students speak in these terms, they will become part of life. In addition, teachers should strive to associate these terms with positive emotion rather than criticism or nagging. The student should hear statements like "That was a good example of fortitude you just did," or "I like your joyousness," or "What a nice parting ritual," or "Wow, you're listing options and choosing," at least four times as often as he hears statements like "Time to get tough and use some fortitude!" When the student is reinforced for positive examples of the skills, this is one of the ways the student comes to be motivated to do more examples of them. If the student can find himself in a climate where both teachers and fellow students value these skills, and are very vocal about their valuing of them, the motivation issue will take care of itself. Of course, creating such a climate in a school is more easily said than done.

Specific activities for motivation and goal-setting

Let's list some of the ideas for motivation toward acquisition of psychological skills.

1. Reading modeling stories, and answering the question, "Was that an example of this, or that?"

2. Having teachers (and, if possible, peers) watch carefully for positive examples, and use immediate social reinforcement, using the terms for the skills, thoughts, feelings, or behaviors as part of the reinforcement.

3. Have teachers notice and acknowledge the positive examples, not just immediately after they occur, but at some regular time of day. This may be called the daily review of the positive examples. This can be done in public.

4. In addition to the positive examples the teacher points out, students can narrate their own positive examples, either that they saw peers doing, or that they did themselves. A student who functions as recording secretary can take down, in an ever-growing text file, the narrative of the positive examples.

5. In addition to writing down these examples, students can reenact the positive examples while other students provide an audience, in brief dramas.

6. In addition to real-life positive examples, students can write their own skills stories, creating positive examples of the psychological skills. These can be

posted or published for others to read. An ever-growing bank of modeling stories can accumulate.

7. The psychological skills scavenger hunt. The students search through works of biography, fictional books, television shows, movies, news reports, or anywhere else for positive models of psychological skills, and they write narratives of these models.

8. Generation of an "internal sales pitch," as a classroom discussion activity. What are the reasons why a certain skill is worth cultivating? What is in it for you, to be good at skill x? What are the advantages to the people you come into contact with, to cultivate skill x? One student can be the recorder, while others verbally contribute ideas. The class can deliberate on several occasions to decide upon a certain number of very cogent reasons to get good at a particular psychological skill, and these can be posted in public places.

9. Public recognition of students for acts of psychological skill.

10. Singing songs that celebrate psychological skills. The most direct example of a song of this sort, for the 16 skills and principles I prefer to emphasize, is "What are the Qualities," which is on the Internet at josephstrayhornmd.com. The words go: "What are

the qualities that make life better? What makes people good? What lets people live in happiness and peace, and brother-and-sisterhood? Productivity, joyousness, kindness, honesty, fortitude; good decisions made every day, nonviolence and not being rude. Friendship-building, self-discipline, loyalty, conservation and self-care; compliance and positive fantasy rehearsal and courage, if you dare."

In addition, there are many other songs that in some way celebrate one or another psychological skill. One useful activity is for students to listen for such songs and to add them to the repertoire for group singing.

Group singing is a great way to build morale, and to build a positive attitude toward what is sung about.

Some learnings from motivational interviewing

Motivational interviewing is used in medicine, psychotherapy, and other helping professions to try to elicit from people what their own goals are, and to help them nurture their own motivation for what is best for them. One of the alternatives that motivational interviewing is meant to supplant is people's all too human tendency to bludgeon one another with highly confrontive and dictatorial statements of "You should do this!" Or, "You're not a good person unless you do this!"

One of the methods of motivational interviewing is listening to the person talk about how their life is going and what they want out of life. The listener uses OARS: open-ended questions, affirmations (or positive feedback), reflections, and summaries of what the speaker has communicated. But the listener is particularly attentive to the utterances the speaker makes that express, or can be paraphrased so as to express, good goals, and wishes or plans to achieve them, otherwise known as "change talk."

Another method is asking someone about a certain goal, and if the person would like to accomplish it, asking what are the reasons the person would like to do so. Sometimes it's good to get both the pros and cons of working toward a certain goal. I have referred to the reasons for working toward a goal as the internal sales pitch.

Motivational interviewers ask people, how strongly do you want to achieve this goal, on a scale of 0 to 10? If the person says, for example, 5, the interviewer might ask, why is the number 5 rather than 0? In other words, what are the reasons for wanting it? This question, in contrast to the question "Why isn't it higher," tends to bring out the person's motives for goal attainment, or "change talk."

Although these methods were developed for one-to-one interactions, some of these can be adapted for written exercises that can be done independently by learners.

Staff happiness as motivator

If teachers and other school staff appear to be miserable, angry, and frustrated a large fraction of the time, it would be natural for students to think, "Why should I buy what they're selling?" Conversely: If the staff and other students in a school create a positive emotional climate; if the staff appear to enjoy life thoroughly; if the

67

students like and admire the staff; if the students have the sense that their efforts are rewarded by improvement in skills that others value; and if the backdrop of all this positive experience is frequent attention to psychological skills, the students will get a very powerful message that psychological skill development is something good that they want to get in on. An individual teacher can contribute to this goal, but the full achievement of a positive emotional climate at schools requires many contributions at all levels.

Chapter 4: Hierarchy-ology

One of the most powerful ideas in education is as follows. We can arrange the challenges a learner faces on the way to competence in a certain skill, in order of difficulty; this ordered list is called a hierarchy; for any learner, at any given time, we want the learner to be able to work at the best point on the hierarchy. More simply put: what we ask students to do should be not too hard, not too easy, but just right. This helps learning to become both successful and pleasant for all involved. On the other hand, when the tasks the learner is focusing on are too hard, frustration results; when the tasks are too easy, boredom sets in. Adjusting the level of difficulty so as to be "just right" is a mark of many successful video games; it's part of what makes these games so addictive. A major task of society is to apply optimum "leveling up" or "leveling down" as in videogames to the skills that improve the human condition rather than those that make one a good "shooter!"

How do we know a "just right" level of difficulty when we see one? I've used the rule of thumb that the learner should be successful on at least 80% of the tasks that the learner tries. Below this frequency of success, we should usually consider an easier task. When do we know when to make the task harder? Learning can often take place well, even with 100% level of success – so-called "errorless" learning. And with very important tasks, such as math facts, it's useful to keep practicing, not just until 100% correct responding is achieved, but until the correct responding is carried out very rapidly. With very accurate

69

and very fast performance, moving to the next higher level is usually warranted. Intuitive judgment by the teacher and feedback from the learner are also involved.

I have seen wonderful things happen when this idea is applied to children who have had trouble learning reading, who enter individual tutoring. The reading program I've outlined in *Manual for Tutors and Teachers of Reading* breaks down the task of learning to read into a series of hierarchically arranged steps. Testing reveals the point on the hierarchy where the learner can be successful at least 80% of the time. The learner begins there, getting lots of positive feedback for successes. The increase in morale that accrues from being able to have success after success energizes the student to succeed more, and to progress up the hierarchy of difficulty. This outcome happens often – of course, not always.

At any given point, if the child finds himself with a task that is unpleasantly frustrating, the tutor performs a very important maneuver: "going down the hierarchy and back up again." For example, suppose the child is trying to sound and blend (i.e. say the separate sounds, then say the whole word) a list of words that share a phonetic principle. If this task is too hard, the tutor asks the child to "sound and blend after me," in other words, to hear the tutor sound and blend and just repeat. If even this task is too hard, the tutor can say the separate sounds of the word and let the student guess the word. If this is too hard, the tutor can simply say the words in the list, one by one, and have the student repeat them. And if the whole list appears too hard, the tutor can move the child down to an easier list to practice with, or move down to activities not involving word lists. And so forth. The fluidity of movement along the hierarchy assures that at any given time, the student will work on something that will yield progress rather than frustration or boredom.

In mathematics, working at the correct level of difficulty is at least as important as with reading. Tests such as the Key Math test, where items are ordered with respect to difficulty level, help us find the easiest mathematical concepts that the child is shaky on. Our instruction should be at that level or below, rather than very far above it.

How is it possible, in a class with, say, 25 students, of widely varying abilities and skill levels, to conduct a traditional class (where all students are focusing on the same activity) while at the same time occupying the correct place on the hierarchy of difficulty for each child? Such a task is clearly impossible. Students either must be divided into groups according to skill level, or individualized methods of education such as one-to-one tutoring, independent study, or computer based exercises that find the correct level for each learner must be employed. This is one of the reasons that individual tutoring has, by and large, resulted in much more effective education than traditional classrooms.

As if teaching each child at the correct level of academic difficulty were not a daunting enough task, we have to take into account, in addition to academic hierarchies, numerous other hierarchies – at least one for each psychological skill. For example: suppose there is a preschool aged child who, when put into a group of children, appears to crave attention but gets it in negative ways such as disrupting what other children are doing or being aggressive. The strategy taken is to move "down the hierarchy" to a situation where the child can more easily do appropriate social interaction, and then work "back up the hierarchy" to the social situation with other children. The "down the hierarchy" situation is in one-on-one interaction with an adult, where the child is shown by modeling and shaping (via the enthusiastic attention of the adult) how to do interactive play with toy people. In another "down the hierarchy" situation, the child at home watches videos of people acting out plays with toy people. When the child is proficient at doing imaginative and interactive play, the child is moved "up the hierarchy" a little bit, by now playing with an adult and one other child who has been coached to reinforce positive play. Gradually the adult withdraws from the interaction, and the "target child" plays with the other child. After positive practice with this, the target child is reintroduced to a free play situation in a group of children, and plays with the adult and the same child with whom play was successful before. Then the child moves further "up the hierarchy" as other children join in, and gradually the adult withdraws, except for frequent enthusiastic social reinforcement for positive play. In the final step back "up the hierarchy," the adult fades the frequency of social reinforcement for positive play to a frequency equal to that of the other children.

Here's another example of the use of hierarchy-ology. A fourth grade child is painfully shy, and fears yet desires positive interactions with other children. When the child sits on the bus or at the lunchroom table with other children, the difficulty level for positive social interaction appears too high. The child is moved "down the hierarchy" by doing a lunchtime tutoring activity. First the child practices with an adult, who teaches the child a very structured way of drilling younger children on math facts or spelling or reading words. The older child is to present the challenge, and if the younger child gets it right, the older child is to say "right!" or "good!" or "you got it!" with a very enthusiastic tone of voice. If the younger child does not get it right, the older child simply tells the correct answer and moves to the next challenge. If the younger child departs from the task and offers some conversation, the tutor is to respond with a "good listening" technique: a facilitation such as "Humh!" or "Oh!" or "I see," or a "reflection" such as, "Sounds like that was fun for you," or "So you're saying, _____." In the first step on the hierarchy, the target child and the adult role play these activities, switching roles back and forth between that of tutor and student. After much successful practice, a child is chosen who will be a reinforcing student, and the target child works with this child. The target child moves up the hierarchy by working with other children who are not quite so easy, and by learning other conversation techniques to use between rounds of drilling. Gradually the child generalizes these techniques to unstructured situations with same-aged peers.

73

Here's another example of the use of hierarchy-ology. A child is disposed to major tantrums. Better frustration-tolerance or fortitude skills is the goal. One way to move "down the hierarchy" with this child is to teach the child to do the "four thought exercise" with an older tutor, using the sort of frustrating situations that tend to cause tantrums for this child. (The "four thought exercise" is to imagine oneself in a situation, and then to come up with sentences to think about that situation that are examples of: 1. not awfulizing, 2. goal-setting, 3. listing options and choosing, and 4. celebrating one's own choice.) But rather than starting here, the child starts even lower on the hierarchy, by working, with an older tutor, through a story that teaches the child the meaning of the types of thoughts. Then the child observes while the tutor models the four-thought exercise with situations chosen at random from a list. Then the child takes turns with the tutor, practicing the four-thought exercise with random situations. Then the situations are chosen so as to more greatly resemble the ones the child has had trouble with. Meanwhile, the child reads, with the tutor, many models of positive use of fortitude skills. Finally the child is asked to keep track of any frustrating situations in real life where the child was able to use fortitude skills. Simultaneously, other people in the child's life repeatedly measure his or her success in fortitude and give feedback to the child at least daily, with celebration and reinforcers tied to good use of fortitude. Then gradually the monitoring and reinforcement are faded over time, constituting the final rise back "up the hierarchy."

74

And here's still another example. A child has a hard time completing homework assignments. The parent goes to the bottom of the homework hierarchy by sitting with the child, asking the child to read aloud each direction and each question, giving prompts and hints as necessary, reinforcing each correct answer the child gives verbally, and then reinforcing each translation of that verbal answer into writing. The parent closely prompts and supervises and reinforces as the student puts the completed homework papers into a backpack that will be taken to school the next day. Once the child is successful at this level, the parent starts to fade the prompts and questions, but continues the social reinforcement. Gradually they move across this stage of the hierarchy to the point where the parent is simply cheering the child on as the child carries out the steps – but the parent is present and watching every moment. In the next stage, the parent is present, but not watching every instant: the child is asked to tell the parent when the child completes a certain amount of work, and the parent checks and reinforces at that time; otherwise the parent is sitting beside the child, working on work of the parent's own. This stage continues for a long time, because it is pleasant for both of them. Gradually the child moves to be able to do the homework while sitting alone, with the parent coming in to check and reinforce periodically. In the next stage, the parent checks only at the completion of all work, and in the next, the parent does not check the child's work at all. The parent continues to intermittently reinforce the child for the child's independent efforts.

A very important part of the artistry of education is constructing hierarchies. The philosophy for the constructor of hierarchies is that 1) there is some entry level for the child that can be successful and pleasant, and 2) there is a series of steps up from that entry level, each of which is not much harder than the previous one, 3) each step gets the student a little closer to being able to do the final goal behaviors, and 4) student and teacher celebrate the completion of each step.

How do skilled hierarchy constructors know how to ply their craft? They do it partly by having general notions of what is easier and what is harder. For example:

1. One-on-one interaction is often easier than group interaction.

2. For inhibited or shy people, structured, specific questions are easier than open-ended questions.

3. For "free spirit" types who love divergent thinking, answering structured, specific questions is more difficult than talking in an unstructured way.

4. Doing difficult activities in imagination or role-playing is easier than doing them in real life.

5. Responding to "hot" or emotion-arousing situations such as frustration or criticism is much easier when not in the "heat of the moment," but during a lesson carried out when calm.

6. Doing difficult activities is much easier immediately after seeing and hearing a model of that activity. (Models can include an adaptive thought sequence, spoken aloud.)

7. Doing an activity for a shorter time, more frequently, is often much easier than doing it for a longer time, less frequently.

8. Doing an activity with frequent positive feedback from someone else is for most people much easier than doing the activity alone.

9. For some very self-conscious people, doing the activity alone is easier than doing it while being watched by someone else.

10. Doing an activity with other people modeling good work on that activity all around you is often much easier than doing the activity alone.

11. Seeing examples and learning to label them correctly is usually easier than being given the concept and being asked to come up with your own examples.

12. Simple sentences, short words, and works with illustrations are easier than complex sentences, longer words, and works without illustrations.

13. Handling a situation you've practiced with is easier than coming up with a response to a situation sprung on you for the first time.

14. Hearing something explained is for some, easier than reading and understanding an explanation; for others, having the written explanation is preferable.

Sometimes a low position on the hierarchy in one of these dimensions permits a higher position on another dimension. For example, the psychoeducational tutoring by telephone program I have directed allows the student to be in an "easy" position on the hierarchy by having someone's one-on-one undivided attention, with frequent feedback, and with lots of positive reinforcement and with turn-taking on the tasks. This allows the child to successfully occupy a higher position on other dimensions, i.e. by reading books with fairly complex language and no pictures. Because the word is the simplest and easiest way to encode information, a child who is able to move to high levels of competence in extracting meaning from the written word has accomplished a major liberation – the child does not need the more expensive and entertaining ways of getting information that other children often need.

Finding a correct position on the hierarchy of difficulty is important for people of all ages, not just with respect to maximum learning and progress, but with respect to happiness and a sense of well-being. Mihaly Csikszentmihalyi, in his book, *Flow*, emphasized that happiness is not so much associated with what we have as with the sense of striving for a goal that is within reach by virtue of being at the correct level of difficulty. Hierarchy-ology is one of the major challenges for optimal education.

Chapter 5: Reading

Reading is a psychological skill

If education is to call itself successful, it should result in learners almost all of whom can read proficiently and who like reading. Unfortunately, large numbers of people in the USA are "functionally illiterate." An exceptionally high fraction of juveniles in the criminal justice system have very poor reading skills. This is a shame, because we know how to teach reading successfully.

We think of psychological skills as those which enable people to be happy and to help others to be happy. Reading skill clearly facilitates both of those goals. Is reading causally related to behavioral outcomes such as disruptive behavior, inattention, and aggression? A great deal of research supports reading and psychological adjustment are causally related in both directions. That is: disruptive, inattentive, aggressive behavior or very painful emotions interfere with learning to read. And for the causal arrow in the other direction: for most children who are substantially behind in reading, school becomes extremely frustrating and unpleasant. Each day of being compelled to go to school represents another day where the realization that "I am failing to do what people expect me to do" is hard to fight off. It is not hard to see why negative behavioral and emotional outcomes ensue.

I said that "most" children who are substantially behind in reading experience school as very unpleasant.

But that's not true for all of them, and the reason is that some schools and teachers successfully practice the principle referred to in the previous chapter: hierarchy-ology. In this case this means that the school and the teachers have clearly in mind a series of steps along the road to reading proficiency, and they adjust the challenges given to the learner so as to be not too hard, not too easy, but in the correct challenge zone.

Let's think about the hierarchies involved in gaining reading competence, and the tasks that advance the learner along the path.

Hierarchies on the way toward reading proficiency

Here are broad stages of reading competence.

1. Oral language development.
2. Phonemic awareness: the ability to put sounds together to make words, and to take words apart into their component sounds.
3. Spatial awareness: skills culminating in the ability to tell b from d, p from q, was from saw, and so forth.
4. Letter-sound correspondence: remembering a certain sound associated with each of the 26 printed letters.
5. Reading words in "word families," or groups of words that use the same phonetic principle.
6. Reading text (from simple to more complex).
7. Improving comprehension.

The skills involved in spelling go along similar hierarchies.

Let's examine a little more thoroughly the hierarchies within each of these stages.

Oral language development

Before learning to read, the foundation is learning to talk and to listen: to understand what people say to you, and to express yourself in words. Of course these skills develop over the life span, but a certain level of competence is a prerequisite for making ideal progress in reading. A measure of such competence is whether the learners can enjoy hearing books read to them. Another is whether they can enjoy back-and-forth conversation. Tests of vocabulary and language competence may be used, but in most cases they are unnecessary to enable the conclusion that the learner is ready to start learning to read.

The low end of the oral language development hierarchy can begin in infancy. As the very young child explores things and manipulates things, the older person uses "tracking and describing," i.e. putting into words what is going on. Tracking and describing might sound like this: "You can make the ball roll! Here it comes, rolling toward me. I'll roll it back back to you. Now it goes up in the air, and now it's over that way. Here it comes back to you again." But there's some silence in between the adult's utterances. And if the young child says anything, even babbling of non-words, the adult responds with tones of enthusiasm, reinforcing the beginning acts of verbalization. As the child develops, the adult says things to the child, is silent long enough for the child to respond, and then responds in a reinforcing way to the child's utterances.

Phonemic awareness

"Here are two pictures: a pig and a man. I'm going to break one of the words into parts, and see if you can put the word back together. See if you can guess which one of these two I'm thinking of. I'm thinking about the puh ih guh." If the learner can point to the picture of the pig, or say "pig," that is beginning level phonemic awareness! To make it one step easier, instead of "puh ih guh," the tutor could have said "puh ig." (The "uh" sound that accompanies consonant sounds spoken in isolation is called a schwa; it's usually good to minimize the schwa, so that the sounds when put together really sound like the word. But often something of a schwa is necessary for the sound to be heard.)

Another low level phonemic awareness challenge is to put together words that are broken apart at the end of a phrase that gives a strong clue of what the word is. "I heard some barking, and it was a duh ŏ guh." "It was hot, so we turned on the fuh aah nnn."

As one goes up the hierarchy, there is practice at blending sounds for words with four or five or even six phonemes, without any clues: "The word is sss tuh rrr ŏ nnn guh."

And at some point the learner practices segmenting, as well as blending. "Can you take the word *go* apart into two sounds?... Right! It's guh oh!" Gradually the learner

82

moves toward segmenting words with more phonemes, such as slick, grind, blank, and so forth.

Many children walk into kindergarten somehow already possessing phonemic awareness. Some children can demonstrate this skill at a very early age. For this reason, it often is not taught systematically in schools. But for those children who lack this skill, moving along a hierarchy of practice tasks can have dramatic positive effects on reading progress. It is obviously impossible to "sound and blend" a word by looking at print, saying the sounds, and blending them together, if you can't blend them when someone else gives you the sounds. Likewise, it's hard to figure out how to spell a word if you can't separate the sounds in it.

Spatial awareness

The phrase "spatial awareness" is the term I give to remembering which of two mirror images is which – for example, being able to say which is b and which is d, which is p and which is q. Learners can progress along a hierarchy to exercise whatever brain regions are in charge of distinguishing mirror images from one another. At the bottom of the hierarchy, the learner can look at pairs of arrows, and just say whether they are pointing in the same or different directions. Then the task can be to look at a series of arrows and decide whether each is pointing to the right or to the left. The learner can look at pairs of pictures that are either identical or mirror images, and say whether they are the same or different. Next might be looking at sets of three images, two of which are identical, and one of which is the mirror image of the other two. The learner selects which one is not like the others. Then the learner can practice with "same or different" with pairs of b and d combinations, or p and q combinations, and then "which is not like the others" with sets like b b d or p q p. The next to last step is looking at b's, d's, p's, and q's and saying whether the "ball" is on the right or left of the "stick." And finally, the learner practices looking at the letters and saying their names or their sounds.

The letters b and d cause lots of difficulty for some learners. Conversely, spending a few hours of concentrated work on distinguishing them can make the reading process lots more pleasant.

Letter-sound correspondence

One of the problems with English is that letters don't always make the same sounds. As an example, someone could argue that the letters ghoti should be pronounced "fish." How? By pronouncing gh as in enough, o as in women, and ti as in nation.

But to make things easy on the beginning reader, we start as if the language were completely phonetic, and teach the sounds that the letters usually make in CVC (consonant-vowel-consonant) words such as box, yet, cat, get, and so forth. Learning 26 associations is enough to start with. As the learners progress, they can learn what sounds th, sh, ph, tion, ight, and so forth usually make. I find that "letter songs" are particularly useful in teaching sound-symbol correspondence. (Some songs that I have recorded are available on the Internet.) Alphabet books or pages with pictures of words beginning with each of the 26 sounds are useful also. In a book of Letter Stories that I wrote, characters who are letters say their sounds and then blend them together to say words that usually help people to prevent some disaster. And in addition to these fun ways toward letter sound correspondence, there are always memorization and drill, starting with small batches of letters to remember the sounds for, and gradually moving toward bigger batches.

Words in word families

Once the student is good at the blending part of phonemic awareness, and at letter-sound correspondence (assisted by spatial awareness), the student is ready for decoding words! The phrase "sounding and blending" means looking at the letters, saying the individual phonemes, and then blending the phonemes to say the word. For example: kuh aah tuh cat! Sounding and blending practice gives a workout to the three previous stages, as well as adding words to the repertoire.

By "word families," we mean words that are grouped so that the phonetic principles do not conflict with one another. For example, mat, pan, jazz, and ram are in one family, whereas stall, halt, small, and talk are in another. For any given list, the a makes the same sound. That way letter sound correspondence does not get contradicted within the same list, and "retroactive and proactive interference" does not keep the learner from remembering.

85

In *Manual for Tutors and Teachers of Reading,* there are 99 lists of one syllable words. In an additional 45 lists, the learner sounds and blends by syllable rather than by individual phoneme.

For "word list work," it's good to give points: 2 points for each word of "sound and blend after the tutor," 2 points for each "sound and blend on your own," and one point for "read off the word without sounding first." These activities provide a little hierarchy for any given list. A study I did found about 1 grade equivalent of decoding progress for each 10,000 word list points – on the average. The progress per point ratio can vary widely among learners. For most children it's not at all difficult to get 100 points in about 10 minutes. This rate would imply that for the average child, one lesson a day, 6 days a week, would yield about 3 grade equivalents progress per year.

We've found it important to keep track of word list points and hold celebrations for milestones such as 1000, 5000, 10,000, and then every 10,000 points thereafter. In OPT, the Organization for Psychoeducational Tutoring, the prize is a certificate, a postcard with a personal message, a $2 bill, plus whatever celebration the family can muster. Keeping track of points lets the student know that each bit of work counts – each bit gets the cumulative total higher. This is a very important concept. The movement from "I got another session over with" to "I got this many points" can make a huge difference.

But the most important reinforcer for word list work is tones of approval coming from the tutor: "Right!… Yes!… You got it!… Good!" The tutor's genuine joy in the student's successes is crucial for the success of the enterprise.

What if the student misses a word? The tutor just models the right answer. For example, if the student sounds and blends the word "huge" as "hug," the tutor might say, "Can you go like this? huh yu juh huge?" Then the student does it, and the tutor gives two points plus approval, and on they go. Lots of children find it fairly aversive to endure long explanations of why their answer was wrong, or being asked to try again without knowing any more than they knew before.

Some educators believe that working on words isolated from their meanings is heresy. To them, this section on word list work would spur heated dispute. In the spirit of debate, I would reply that 1) sounding and blending, and then reading off, words in isolation is of proven effectiveness in increasing decoding skills; 2) the amount of time per day that the student is asked to do this activity is only somewhere between 5 and 15 minutes; 3) drill and practice are useful in sports, music, dance, mathematics, typing, and nearly all other areas of expertise, and those who are used to it have big advantages in life; 4) when an enthusiastic companion is cheering your every success and keeping track of your cumulative achievement, the activity can be, rather than pure self-discipline practice, a success experience that is fun.

Text reading

As soon as the learner's decoding skills have reached a certain point through word list work, the learner is ready to start reading connected text, e.g. stories. These should be constructed so as to consist of the sorts of words the learner has been able to read so far. The "primer stories" in *Manual for Tutors and Teachers of Reading* are meant to be very first stories, and of course there are many other sources for books low on the hierarchy.

Just as with keeping track of word list points, it's useful to keep track of "text units," and to celebrate milestones with these.

In our experience, it's far more favorable for the tutor and learner to *take turns* reading brief stories, or reading the pages or paragraphs or illustrated panels of stories, than it is for the learner to do all the work. This lets the tutor model how to read expressively, lets the learner listen as well as read, allows the tutor to model enjoyment of reading aloud, and makes the interpersonal climate feel more egalitarian rather than one where there's an order-giver and an order-performer. We refer to such turn-taking as "alternate reading." It is a great activity for education.

When text reading begins, the question immediately comes up, "Why should a child want to read this? Is this text even more boring than word lists?" Fortunately, it appears to me that stories wherein it makes a lot of difference how psychologically skillfully someone acts, tend to capture children's interest.

Tasks for comprehension

What do you need to do, to comprehend what you have read? You need to:
1. Be able to call out the words. (decoding)

2. Know what the words mean. (vocabulary)

3. Be able to combine the meanings of the individual words to grasp the meanings of larger combinations of them, i.e. sentences, paragraphs, chapters…. (working memory and attention)

All of these skills improve with practice!

The "programmed format" discussed earlier in this book gives comprehension practice by presenting a summary question to the learner after each section of approximately 150-300 words.

For text that is not in the programmed format, comprehension can be practiced by doing the "reflections exercise" with each paragraph, i.e. giving a short summary or paraphrase of it.

To probe comprehension, or not to probe? There's something to be said for just getting so involved in what you are reading that you don't want to interrupt yourself with comprehension probes, because you can't wait to get to the next part. Comprehension probes are definitely not required. However, they can provide learners with a challenge that gives the tutor the opportunity to celebrate the learner's success, and sometimes they can make the reading much more pleasant than just going straight through the reading.

Spelling

Learning correct spelling in English requires lots and lots of memorization. But getting good at the segmenting part of phonemic awareness helps greatly in the beginning stages. And it seems most sensible to take on lists of spelling words that are grouped just as they are grouped in the word families for reading, where words with the same phonetic principle are learned together. As with reading, that way memories won't interfere with one another so much.

Older students as reading tutors for younger students

Every one of the tasks described above can be conducted by older children with younger children – provided that they have enough training, and enough role-played practice. One of the best methods of tutor training is for the student to have experienced such tutoring themselves. My own daughters, when they were ages 8 and 9, respectively, began tutoring other children quite successfully, after having gone through the curriculum themselves. At the beginning there were large inputs of supervision and monitoring; as time went by, they became more and more able to do the job independently.

The vision of older children, paired with younger ones, giving lots of approving and enthusiastic feedback, while the younger child gets practice in the most crucial academic skill, and both of them feel successful in accomplishment, is a vision that some day may become reality on a large scale.

Dyslexia

As mentioned earlier, children differ widely in the rate of reading progress made per unit work invested. I have worked with, and have supervised work with, substantial numbers of children for whom reading was more difficult than for other children. And this set includes several children who met any set of criteria for "dyslexia" or "specific learning disorder in reading." My experience has been that such children can get to be proficient in reading, with instruction that: 1) pays close attention to the foundation skills of phonemic awareness, spatial awareness, and letter-sound correspondence, and does not cease working on these skills before they are mastered, 2) pays close attention to hierarchy-ology, and works at the best level for the child, ignoring the level for age-mates (and helping the child to ignore that also); and 3) makes repetitive practice fun enough that the child can carry out several to many times as much practice as most other learners require. The activities practiced are the same ones that faster learners use.

Chapter 6:Attribution and Prophecy

The phenomenon of self-fulfilling prophecy

Sometimes it does appear that predicting something or expecting it to happen actually helps make it happen. If enough people expect the stock market to go down, then it probably will (in the short run at least). If it is widely predicted that a movie will be a blockbuster, then the movie's chances are helped by the prediction itself. If someone goes into a musical performance fully expecting that he will go blank in the middle of the performance and he will be greatly embarrassed and mortified, the chances of his doing so are enhanced by anxiety. If a mother says repeatedly to a child, "You're going to wind up in prison before you're 18, just like that no good father of yours did," the chances that the child will fulfill that prophecy are probably increased.

When you say to a child, "You are shy," you are attributing to the child the trait of being shy. Whenever you attribute a trait to someone, you in a sense make a prophecy. When a child hears, "You are shy," the meaning he gathers is that he will continue to act the way a shy person acts. On the other hand, if you should say to the child, "I think you can find some bravery within yourself to handle this," you are attributing to the child the trait of bravery. Attribution, then, is the process of talking about what traits and abilities child does or does not have.

Why might the prophecies that attributions make turn out to be self-fulfilling sometimes? Perhaps because someone comes to imagine himself as a certain sort of person, and tends to fantasy rehearse the thoughts and behaviors that go along with being that sort of person. Perhaps the belief that the person is a certain sort of way tends to make the child scared to try being a different way: for example if I am really shy, it makes sense that risking being socially outgoing may be more dangerous for me than for other people. Perhaps people get an image of themselves, and they feel secure when they do things consistent with that image, and feel uncomfortable breaking out of the mold they've created for themselves.

This chapter has to do with the question: how can we make attributions and possibly self-fulfilling prophecies in such a way as to be honest, yet maximize our chances of being helpful to the student? We don't want to shelter children from the truth about their negative behaviors, but we want to speak of the negative behaviors in such a way as to imply that they are not permanent.

Using attribution after undesirable behavior

Does the fact that attributions influence behavior mean that you have to tell your student that he's perfect in every way? Imagine saying, for example, about the very shy student, "Oh, he's so outgoing, he just goes up and talks to people, and is totally relaxed about it." This type of utterance would probably have the main effect of letting your student know that you are a bold-faced liar.

Attributions need to be honest—as, by the way, do all other utterances made to the student.

However, if the student is not very good at doing something, you can still talk about the things the student needs to improve, but with the idea that the student can improve them rather than that the student has fixed traits that are undesirable. How do you do that?

For any sentence that anyone says to a student that says, "You are bad in some way," you can change that into a sentence that says, "When you get better in this way, positive things will happen." For example, we can translate

"You're not kind."

into

"When you start doing more kind things for the people in your life, they'll like being with you more."

Here are some other forms attribution, forms to translate negative attributions into:

1. I really will like it when he (or you) _____.
2. I expect that he (or you) might _____.
3. If you (or he) _____, things will be better, because _____.
4. He hasn't learned to _____ yet, but I hope he will soon.

It's helpful to practice saying things in that way rather than calling the student bad.

Here's an example of a translation:

"He's not a writer. He loves to read, but writing is not his cup of tea."

How about translating that into, "It will really be great when his love of writing develops and catches up with his love of reading."

If you were the student, and you heard the second, perhaps you would grow your writing skills a bit faster.

Attribution after desirable behavior

Attribution is of positive traits after desirable behavior is another side of the attribution coin. Suppose a student does something nice for someone else. It is very reinforcing for the adult to say, "I really do appreciate that nice thing that you did. You brightened up my day." But suppose the adult says, "It made me feel really good to see you doing that, because it showed me what a kind person you are becoming." This goes farther than communicating the effects on the speaker; it also attributes to the student the trait of kindness which is developing and unfolding more and more as time goes on.

When someone sees positive behaviors from another, it's sometimes possible to interpret them as signs of the unfolding of lasting positive traits.

Here are a couple of examples. An adult is teaching the student some math concepts, and the student catches on. A "pure reinforcer" would be "Right! Good thinking!" Reinforcement with an added attribution would be, "Right! I think you're developing some real skill in math!"

The adult observes the student with other students. The previously shy student is having fun meeting people and talking with people. The student comes back to chat with the adult a while. A "pure reinforcer" would be, "Wow, you're really getting to meet a lot of new people!" An added attribution would be, "You're getting friendlier and more outgoing with people all the time, did you know that?"

There are people who believe that we should skip attributions of positive traits and stick to comments about specific positive behaviors. One reason for this is that there are some people who do not want to be judged, in positive or negative ways, and skipping positive attributions avoids offending such people. On the other hand: Traits, or habits of thinking, feeling, or behaving, do exist, and people tend to think in terms of them, rather than seeing each behavior in isolation. And as is apparent to anyone who chooses which employees to hire, whom to marry, whom to accept a car ride with, or whom to make a loan to, we make judgments about people based on their traits. Those who take great offense at being judged, positively or negatively, might be well advised to get over it! But until they succeed, teachers can take their wishes not to be judged into account.

Attributions part 3: Prophecies "out of the blue"

You don't have to wait until the student does something good or bad to make an attribution or prophecy. Consider the following examples.

A student has a problem with screaming when frustrated. The teacher and the student are talking. The teacher says, "I just thought of something that made me smile." The student says "What was it?" The teacher says, "I thought to myself that some day there may be a day when we both realize that you haven't raised your voice in frustration or anger for months, and where you've gotten into a habit of speaking in a calm and quiet voice. I'll say to myself, 'Wow, am I glad how my student has matured!' That will really feel good. How should we celebrate when that day comes, I wonder?"

A student hasn't learned to read yet. The adult says, "You may not believe it now, but some day, you're going to be able to pick out any book on this book shelf and read it easily. What a happy scene! I hope I get to see it myself. I'd be so happy for you, I'd think to myself, 'Now she can read anything she wants! Whole new worlds are open to her!'"

A student and a teacher are talking. The teacher says, "I wonder what life is going to be like for you in a few years, let's say when you're graduating from this school. I hope you'll have lots of friends that you have fun with. I hope people think of you and say, 'That's really a kind person, who loves other people.' I hope you'll be getting real joy out of learning lots of new things at school."

These prophecies have the effect of not only giving hope that the desired end will take place, but also defining the reaching of the goal as a very joyous occasion. If the student can start seeing a joyous vision of reaching the goal, the student is much more likely to reach it sooner.

Chapter 7: Modeling

It is a basic characteristic of the human brain to store in memory images of what other human beings do, and to access these images when choosing one's own behaviors. What we do is greatly influenced by what we see and hear others do; many studies, as well as ordinary observation, establish this fact without doubt. Imitation learning is a prime influence on what people do.

One of the goals of education, accordingly, should be the laying down, in the memory banks of children and youth, as many as possible of the types of positive models that will be most useful to them in life – the models of productivity, joyousness, kindness, honesty, fortitude, and the other psychological skills.

One of the most robust findings from social learning oriented psychology is that models can influence behavior even when they are fictitious, and when the observer knows that they are fictitious.

How well do schools do at helping students accumulate memories of positive behaviors, thoughts, and feelings? Courses in literature for middle school and high school students reflect the fact that the literature to which people gravitate is not written for the primary purpose of showing positive ways of living. Here's a brief sample of some of the classic literature I read during high school:

Albert Camus, *The Stranger*: The main character commits a senseless murder, without empathy for the victim.

Fyodor Dostoevsky, *Crime and Punishment*: The main character commits a senseless murder, and wrestles with the implications during the rest of the story.

Flannery O'Connor, "A Good Man is Hard to Find": An "outlaw" murders a group of people on vacation, without a logical motive.

Edgar Allen Poe, "A Cask of Amantillado": The main character seals someone in a brick vault, so that the person will die slowly; revenge is the motive.

Edgar Allen Poe, "The Tell-Tale Heart": The main character performs a senseless murder of an old man because he doesn't like the way the man's eye looks. He gives himself away to the police because he hears a heart beating.

William Golding, *Lord of the Flies*: Boys stranded on an island regress to savagery, killing one of their comrades in a frenzy of bullying.

William Shakespeare, *Hamlet*: The major characters (The elder Hamlet, Hamlet, Polonius, Claudius, Gertrude, Laertes, and Ophelia) *all* end up dead from either homicide or suicide.

Richard Connell, "The Most Dangerous Game": The protagonist encounters, and eventually kills, someone who hunts other people for the fun of it.

Sophocles, *Oedipus Rex*: When the protagonist finds out that he has killed his father and married his mother, he blinds himself.

John Steinbeck, *Of Mice and Men*: A protagonist with intellectual disability accidentally kills animals and a human being by not knowing his own strength; the other protagonist, his friend, shoots and kills him to protect him from a lynch mob.

Herman Melville, *Moby Dick*. A whaling ship captain becomes obsessed with destroying a particular whale, to point of sacrificing his own life and that of almost all his crew in the quest.

F. Scott Fitzgerald, *The Great Gatsby*: Gatsby is in love with and starts an affair with Daisy, who is the wife of Tom Buchanan; Tom is at the same time having an affair with Myrtle. Daisy ends up running over Myrtle with a car; Myrtle's husband, thinking Gatsby was the driver, kills Gatsby and then himself.

These works all tell us something about the human condition, and they illustrate extremely skillful use of words. And the study of psychopathology through literature as well as through science can be very useful. Of course these works should not be banned. But they also clearly illustrate that the literature we consider great and compel young people to read, usually contains very bad models. Exactly the same conclusion can be reached from an examination of popular literature and movies, history, the news, songs, videogames, and other sources of narratives of human behavior. Models of what *not* to do are plentiful, even unavoidable!

Accordingly, if we wish to also expose children and youth to positive models, we must work at it. We must search through literature, history, children's real-life experience, and through children's own imaginations for the best models that we can conjure up. Then we must collect these, index them by age and other variables, catalog them, and make their storage and retrieval easy and quick and inexpensive.

The bank of positive models

Please imagine the following project for a school. The teachers and the students collaborate to collect a large bank of positive models, many for each of the 16 psychological skills groups, and many for each of the 62 individual psychological skills. This bank will be continually revised and added to.

The first task of the collectors is to read from existing stores of positive models, so as to learn to connect the psychological skill labels to the concrete models, to use the language in a common way. Then the collectors search through other sources, and propose additions to the corpus. Editors make decisions about whether a certain addition is worthy of being included. For revisable work, other editors hone the work until it is most worthy of inclusion.

Once included in the corpus, the material becomes used in the teaching of reading and literature. Any revisable work becomes used in the teaching of writing. And the entire corpus is drawn upon in the teaching of psychological skills.

What are sources of positive models to get the project started? My book, *Illustrated Stories That Model Psychological Skills*, presents positive models of the 16 skills for young readers. My book, *Programmed Readings for Psychological Skills*, starts with many brief vignettes modeling the 16 skill groups, and ends with brief vignettes modeling all 62 psychological skills. These, as well as the examples in the other books I've written on psychological skills, can be a starting point. The Heartwood Institute, which unfortunately no longer is operative, presented a collection of published illustrated books modeling love, respect, honesty, and other psychological skills. The *Value Tales* series by Spencer and/or Ann Donnegan Johnson (now out of print) presented illustrated biographies that illustrate values such as patience, kindness, determination, self-discipline, and others. Other collections, such as Bennett's *The Book of Virtues* and *The Moral Compass*, Greer & Kohl's *A Call to Character*, stories for children by Richard Gardner, and the anthology, *Values,* by Michael Spring, are examples of compilations purposely presenting positive models.

Once students are very familiar with what a positive model looks like, they are assigned, many times, to find or create positive models that are candidates for admission to the positive model bank. Such models may be snippets from works which are not meant to provide positive models – small bits of interaction, a particular decision at a choice point, that is imitation-worthy. Students are asked to search through fictional works, biographies, movies, television shows, and real-life events in their experience and those of others, that meet the criteria for imitation-worthiness.

Thus, one brief assignment to students is simply to search for, and report upon, a positive model. The student's production is a brief piece of writing, summarizing the situation and the choice point with which someone was faced, and then the behavior and as much as is known of the thoughts and emotions of the person in that choice point. Finally, the student can mention what positive effects the person's action had, and which psychological skill(s) it is an example of.

The psychological skills book report

An activity connected with this quest is the psychological skills book report. The students write a report on a book, analyzing it in terms of what positive and negative examples of psychological skills were enacted by the characters. For the negative examples, what would they have been better off doing – in other words, what would have been a positive example of the skills in question? What negative impact upon the character or other people did the action have? For the positive examples: which actions are examples of which psychological skills? Did the action make a positive impact on the character or other people by luck, or by intention? Or was it an imitation-worthy action, which by luck, brought about bad consequences? Are there exemplary actions in the book which deserve to be anthologized into the bank of positive models?

Of course, the format for analyzing narratives can be applied not only to books, but also to short stories, television shows, plays, biographies, historical accounts, news stories, or first-hand experience.

The positive models interview

Another activity included in this quest is the "positive models interview." The student's job is to find some older person, or even a same-age peer, who is willing to be interviewed, and to pose to that person the questions: Of the choices you have made in your life, of which do you feel most proud? Which of your actions do you feel are most imitation-worthy? Which, looking back upon them, are most glad for having done? Which do you think would constitute the best models for people interested in how to live proficiently?

A second part of the positive models interview is as follows. The student poses the same question, not just about the interviewee's actions, but the actions of other people that have affected that interviewee. What has someone done that has affected you positively? What has someone done that was a good decision, that enriched your life? Of the actions other people have taken that have affected you, or that you have witnessed, which would constitute the best additions to an anthology of positive models?

The celebrations diary

The written version of the celebrations exercise is a fertile source of positive models. In the celebrations exercise, the student answers the question, "What is something that you have done, that you are glad to have done? Please describe very concretely the situation you were in, and your thoughts, emotions, and behaviors as you responded to the situation. Please identify the psychological skill or skills that your action was an example of."

A similar written assignment asks students to "celebrate someone else's choice" rather than their own choice. This assignment might read as follows:

"Please write about an exemplary, imitation-worthy action you have seen or heard about someone else's performing. Please make clear the situation to which the person responded. Please describe the person's actions specifically. If you do not know the exact words, thoughts, and emotions of the person, you might guess as to what these are, making it clear in your writing that you are guessing rather than knowing for sure. Please identify the psychological skill or skills that this action was an example of."

The celebrations of some students can be the models for others. Throughout this project, the effort is to collect the best examples and to make them available for dissemination. The more times positive examples can go through the minds of the students, the more psychological growth is occurring.

Writing skills stories

Of course, a never-ending source of positive models is the creative imagination of the students themselves. Students should be encouraged to imagine a very wide range of situations for their characters to find themselves in. The assignment might read like this:

"Using your own imagination, write a 'skills story.' Keep in mind that the primary purpose of this story is not entertainment, but the presentation of a model that is useful, exemplary, imitation-worthy. (If it happens to be entertaining as well, that is fine also.) Please make very clear what situation your main character is in. Keep in mind that your model may be more useful if you present not only the behaviors, but also the thoughts and emotions of your character. After you finish the story, please make for the reader a "comprehension probe" in which you ask the reader which of two psychological skills the story exemplifies. Try to pick the skills so that the story does exemplify one of them, and does not exemplify the other."

Stories and plays from the "Play Plots"

In my book, *Plays That Model Psychological Skills*, I present a set of basic plot outlines.

These can be used in various ways. I originally used them for purposes of improvisational drama with children. The child and the preceptor would take the basic plot outline and start acting, embellishing the general plot with rich specific details from their own imaginations. Examples of general plots are as follows: One person is trying to find something, and the other helps them find it. One person is afraid of doing something, and the other helps them use relaxation or fantasy rehearsal or some other method to get over the fear. Two people work very hard together to accomplish something, and the news reporting gives only one of them credit for it. Together they figure out how to respond.

These basic plots can be used as rubrics upon which modeling stories are built. The assignment might be:

The following is a "play plot".... Please write a story or a play, using this general plot as your rubric, but fleshing it out with specific details from your own imagination. Keep in mind that with any one play plot, there is an infinite number of plays or stories that could be created from it. Create one that you like."

What are positive models? Debates

One person's positive model is another person's negative model. For example: one person sees someone's climbing Mount Everest as a model of great courage; another sees it as a nonproductive activity, an unnecessary risk, a bad example of both self-care and careful decision-making. One person sees a person's rise to championship in boxing as a great example of self-discipline and courage; another sees the same behaviors as terrible examples of the skills of nonviolence and self-care and kindness. One person greatly admires someone who raised himself from poverty to become an action and adventure movie star; another person feels that this person has presented a deplorable model of positive fantasy rehearsal.

The fact that people can disagree on what is good, proficient, ethical, and psychologically healthy is no surprise: people have been doing so throughout history. In fact, competitive idea-slinging in this realm is a competitive sport, known as debate. Through debate, the competitive spirit of young people is often harnessed in the service of learning to use articulate expression and persuasive language. Debate also can provide a way of practicing perspective-taking: what do you do in your mind when you are assigned to defend a position you don't really believe in? You learn to see things from the point of view of those people who do believe in that position, if only temporarily.

Accordingly, here is a writing assignment that can be repeated many times:

"From a work of literature, history, current events, or any other source, select a model of thought, feeling, and behavior that some people could see as positive and others might see as negative. Conduct, in writing, a debate upon this example. Present the argument of the person who is in favor of this model, in a brief speech. (This person presents the 'pros' of the behavior.) Then present the argument of the person who is against the model. (This person presents the 'cons' of the behavior.) If you want, you can have rebuttal speeches, in which the two characters respond to the points that the other has made. Attempt to make the best case you can for each point of view." Some people who come to mind as exemplars of behavior that might make for good debates are: Alexander "the Great," Catherine "the Great," Joan of Arc, J. Robert Oppenheimer, Muhammad Ali, Sylvia Plath, Socrates, Aristotle, Bill Clinton, Marie Curie, Jimmy Carter, Bill Gates – and many others. The debate is not over whether the person was praiseworthy or not – the debate is over some specific behaviors that the person did, and whether those behaviors constitute predominantly a positive or negative model.

In some circumstances it may be useful to have a spoken debate, according to the usual format, where argumentation is a spectator sport. In other circumstances this may defeat the purpose of helping students to think most clearly about the ethical issues involved.

Here's a way to have a noncompetitive psychological skills debate. Instead of having one team present one side and one team present the other, both teams present both the "affirmative" and the "negative" sides to the question. Rather than voting which side did best, the audience for the presentation votes for which side of the issue seemed best supported by the presentations.

Storage and editing of positive models

Some positive models that students find or create will be worth reading by other students. Some will be so good that they deserve to be preserved in an anthology.

Let's visualize that when a model is deemed, by a teacher, to be good enough for the anthology, it is entered into computer storage and sent to a central "editor's office."

The editors are responsible for making sure that there are not errors in grammar, punctuation, spelling, or sentence structure. The editors, of course, should be students, working under the close supervision of writing teachers. The editors should send the corrected copy back to the author, so that the author can accept or reject the changes.

Once the final copy is completed, it is inserted into the proper anthology under the proper classification. I envision one anthology for celebrations, one for skills stories, one for positive models from literature, one for models from interviews, one from history, and so forth. Within any given anthology, the psychological skills form the outline of the models.

Models of models

Assignments to find or imagine or recount positive models are not easy. But they become easier for students if they have seen how other students have responded to the same assignment. Thus the growing bank of models produced by student work becomes useful not only in exemplifying positive psychological skills, but in showing other students how to do the assignments.

Making tests of reading comprehension

Why does nearly every standardized achievement test, from early grade school through graduate school, contain a very prominent section on reading comprehension? Because this skill is obviously one of the most useful and important ones that an educated person can possibly acquire. How is reading comprehension tested? By presenting passages of written work, and then asking various types of questions about those passages. Almost any test-prep book, from Spectrum Test Prep and Scoring High books for grade schoolers, to SAT and ACT test prep books for high schoolers, to the MCAT for those wanting to go to med school, gives examples of the types of questions test-makers ask about the passages.

To prepare students to ace reading comprehension tests, as well as to give them practice in writing, as well as to give them practice at not just reading a passage, but understanding it well enough to find the major "question-worthy" points within it, the following assignment may be given.

"The passage that you have been given is one from our 'Positive Model Anthology.' You have also been given a copy of a portion of a standardized test of reading comprehension, in which the test-makers present a reading passage for the testee to read, and then a set of multiple-choice questions about the passage. You are also given a copy of the answers, and explanations of why the answers are correct. Your assignment is to make up four similar multiple-choice questions about the passage from our Positive Model Anthology. After your set of questions, please write an answer key, with a brief explanation of why the correct answer is correct and why the others are not."

The questions asked about a passage should be models, not primarily of test-making expertise, but of questions an active mind generates and finds answered while reading. The reading comprehension test questions and explanations that the teacher deems most worthy are sent to an editorial board, for editing, and back to the author for approval. These then are also collected in an anthology of reading comprehension tests. With the aid of widely available reading level indicators, these passages can be arranged in order of difficulty, so as to gradually create a growing anthology of positive models that has been fitted with "comprehension probes."

Then, of course, these reading comprehension tests can be used to give students much practice in reading comprehension, at the same time that they are importing positive models into their memory banks.

Writing for other people to read

Often, students' written assignments are read only by a teacher, and assigned a grade. The grade is entered into a grade book permanently, but the composition itself is ignored. This is writing as a performance test, and it is not totally without benefit. But a whole new realm of pleasure and meaning in writing comes when the students see their writing as possibly preserved and read perhaps by many other people, who will be enlightened by their work. In this case, writing is not just to prove oneself; it is an act of kindness and giving to other people. It is a cooperative act and not just part of competition for grades. This is the perspective that makes writing fun for most real-life writers. They envision the readers out there who will be affected by their words, and this vision keeps them going.

This new perspective on writing is achieved by the Bank of Positive Models project. When the project is done well, students really are writing for other students, and for the public at large, with the collaboration of their teachers. They are involved in an extremely worthy goal, capable of helping many people. This can arouse hopes that the pen can be mightier than the sword. (Or: the keyboard can be mightier than the bombs.)

Just in case the readers "out there" may not get around to reading the writings that are particularly

112

noteworthy, students can read to each other. Here is the way an assignment might read:

"You have, in class, heard excerpts from recorded books, read by professional actors. You have noticed how the actor gives great expression to the work, without overacting. You have noticed how the actor uses different intonation for different characters. Please take the modeling story that you have written, and decide very carefully how it should best be read. We will divide into groups of 2 or 3, and you will read your story to your classmates. I, your teacher, will walk around and listen to parts of the stories being read. I will select certain students to read their stories again, to the rest of the class."

Dramatic activities for positive models

The Bank of Positive Models can include another important type of work: scripts for actors. Rather than prose fiction, positive modeling plots can be created in the form of lines spoken by the characters and stage directions. An important subset of these is plays with two characters; in this case, the play can be enacted in one-to-one tutoring.

Improvisation of modeling plays, or converting prose stories into plays, is another classroom activity. For example, the teacher might pick examples from the Bank of Positive Models and distribute them to pairs or small groups of students. The students have a brief time to discuss, decide, and rehearse, after which they are to perform a play enacting that positive model. They do this first for themselves. Then, as time permits, groups of students who want to can put on their plays for the whole class.

Improvisational drama works best with certain ground rules. First, anyone can play anyone else, regardless of age, gender, race, etc. Second, if there is a "prop" needed that is not present, the actor simply remarks upon the imaginary object, staying in role if possible, getting out of role briefly if necessary. If there are actions that are unclear when acted out without props, the actor simply describes his actions while doing them. For example: "Let's see: let me get this can off the shelf, and here's the can opener, I'm starting to open it up. But what's this I see? There's a strange color here! Maybe this is poisonous now. How can I find out?" Third, if there are more characters than there are actors, the actors can switch roles simply by saying, "Now I'm (name of the other character)." Fourth, the actors are encouraged to do "soliloquies" so that you can hear their thoughts and emotions as well as to see their actions. Figuring out how to make it clear what is going on, when there are no costumes or props, is a great exercise in perspective-taking. The actor has to take the perspective, not just of the character, but also of the audience, and to supply the missing information that straight acting will not give the audience.

As with written models, acted out models can be captured by video media and preserved for others to watch. We can envision assemblies in which students gather to watch videos of other students acting out modeling dramas – a very fun way to spend school time.

In all of these activities, there's the effort to help students see themselves as on an important mission: to create positive models for consumption by a world that needs them desperately and in which they are in short supply. Can school staff convince students of the importance of this mission? Can they even convince themselves? If these challenges can be successfully met, the results may be amazing.

Models of tutoring, captured on video or in writing

One of the major themes of this book is that when students are tutors for other students, both students learn. Furthermore, the skills needed for expert tutoring are the same interpersonal and dependability skills most vital for other types of human relations.

The power of imitation learning should be harnessed in the service of teaching students to tutor other students. Many such sessions should be video recorded; many others should be audio recorded and transcribed into printed words. As in other endeavors to create a bank of positive models, a similar project creates a bank of positive tutoring models. Positive models are submitted to teachers who select models to be submitted to editors. The transcription of audio records or video records of tutoring sessions is another writing and spelling activity that constitutes "writing for someone else, not just writing for a grade." The most important concepts of how to tutor well get captured on video and print records, in a growing anthology on how to tutor well.

Analysis of negative models

As I mentioned at the beginning of this chapter, many of the works that high schoolers are asked to read present very negative models of human behavior. Although I believe that the "media diets" of children, youth, and adults are way too heavily skewed toward models of how not to behave, I am not advocating avoidance or censorship of negative models in fiction, and of course not in history or current events. But I suggest the following as questions for students to ponder, when reading about human mistakes, failures, and unethical actions:

1. What were the consequences of the action that the person took, that lead us to classify the action as wrong or mistaken or misguided? How did the action affect the person themselves, and how did it affect other people?

2. What do we think went on in the mind of the character that led them to make this mistake? What were they trying to accomplish? What was their motive? Do we know anything about how this motive came about?

3. Proficiency in which psychological skills, and adherence to which ethical principles, would have prevented the mistake?

4. Can we think of influences that would have helped the person not to have made this mistake? Can we generalize the influences we think of to the question of how to make a better society?

116

5. What parallels are there between this mistake and other ones that are going on in the present world? In other words, are people making similar sorts of mistakes?

6. Can we extract, from our analysis of this mistake, some learnings that may be helpful to us, the people who attend this school?

Chapter 8: Ways to Practice Psychological Skills

Practice of positive patterns of thinking, feeling, and behaving, that are appropriate to the situation in question, is a *sine qua non* of developing psychological skills. This chapter presents some important ideas about practice.

Self-discipline practice through academic drills

Self-discipline is the skill of working toward a worthy goal, even though there are other alternatives to do that are more pleasant. A way of practicing self-discipline is to push oneself to greater and greater output of labor, whether physical or mental: to develop greater *work capacity.* Students will benefit from realizing that they may gain as much from developing work capacity as they gain from the academic skills they are practicing.

I could not agree more with those who point out that education which consists only of drudgery and drilling, the benefits of which students are clueless, is bad practice. On the other hand, including carefully titrated amounts of drill and practice, interspersed among more creative activities, teaches children crucial academic skills as well as the more important skill of self-discipline.

It is desirable in mathematics to have proficiency in the elementary facts of addition, subtraction, multiplication, and division. In doing word problems, it is possible to drill very usefully in deciding which operation to do upon two quantities in order to answer a question stated in words. In spelling English words, much time must be devoted to practice and memorization; the same goes for learning vocabulary. Much practice is useful in gaining proficiency in touch typing. Lots of practice is useful in learning to recognize and correct grammatical errors. All of these activities can be the content for self-discipline drills.

Computerized drills

Much of educational computer software has been designed to attempt to make practice of academic skills fun. There is another genre, however, which eliminates all distraction from animated characters, music, scenes, and so forth, and presents task after task of academic work. Programs are constructed so that the maximal number of rehearsals per minute that the user is capable of may be carried out, with no waiting upon the software. The program gives feedback and keeps records both of the accuracy and the speed of the respondent.

There are "no-frills" programs of this sort for vocabulary, math facts, math problem-solving, touch typing, spelling, and certain aspects of English grammar. Such programs can be written and revised by students themselves who are studying computer programming. Ideally, programs give feedback not only on the learner's performance for a given trial, but how the performance compares with that learner's previous trials.

Speed and accuracy

Perhaps the most central idea of those educational theorists who index their work under the term "precision teaching" is the following: Neural energy, and short term memory, are finite resources. Complex mental operations can be broken down into simpler component skills. The more the component skills can become automatic, the less of neural resources they will consume, leaving more neural resources available for the demands of the problem. And the way to make those component skills automatic is to practice them until they can be done at top speed.

For example: in mathematics: solving several step word problems involving algebra is a complex operation. But if the elementary math facts, the steps in doing the same thing to both sides of an equation to solve for a variable, and the finding of the correct operation to get a third quantity given two others, have all become practiced to the point of automaticity, the student will have more memory and processing power available to plotting out the series of steps necessary to solve this particular problem. The student who is struggling to remember whether and how to multiply and divide whole numbers can't focus enough attention on the other demands of the problem. Thus sometimes the best way to help a student at word problems is to go back and practice the component skills until they can be done very fast.

As a second example: writing a well organized composition is a complex task. The student who has learned either keyboarding or handwriting, spelling, grammar and punctuation, and sentence combining (i.e.

taking two or more short sentences and combining them into one), to the point of fluency and automaticity, is much better equipped to handle the complex task of figuring out something to say and saying it coherently. If the component skills are all shaky, the student is often trying to juggle too many tasks at once.

But teachers must be careful: children can be traumatized by speed drills, especially those done in front of someone else and where performance can be contrasted with that of others. It is essential that: 1) speed drills should never be done in a way that the student is embarrassed in front of other people; 2) performance should be compared to the student's past performance, not to that of other students, and 3) before even trying for speed, the student should be comfortable with nearly 100% accurate, though slow, performance. (Some education theorists disagree with the last of these statements. But it stands to reason that we want to practice doing things the right way rather than the wrong way, and going for speed too early risks rapid practice of incorrect performance.)

In-person social reinforcement

We must apply the art of hierarchy-ology to academic drills. If we could count on all students to sit down alone at the computer and to do academic practice programs for long periods of time and with high productivity, much of the job of education would have been finished already. But it is much easier for a student to do this when a real human being is present as preceptor. The preceptor fulfills the function of providing social reinforcement. When the student finishes with a unit of practice, the preceptor notes the performance, celebrates if it is a significant improvement over past performance, helps the student to accurately graph the performance, and uses "tones of approval" in proportion to the student's improvement over the past. The preceptor helps the student answer the question: if this was a good performance, how did the student do it? If this was not a very good performance, what can be learned from it? The preceptor then tries to build up some suspense for the next performance. Will the student be able to break the record? Will this be the occasion for the best performance of the student's life so far? The preceptor functions to set the stage, much as does the pregame patter that sportscasters do before an athletic contest.

The role of preceptor for these tasks is one that may be well performed by older students. The older student is practicing interpersonal skills, as the younger student practices self-discipline and academic skills.

As students move along the hierarchy toward greater and greater autonomy, they become able to participate in academic drills independently. But it may be useful always to retain a social context whenever possible. A stage further along on the hierarchy of difficulty is for two students to be partners in the drilling. They sit near each other, and each of them drill; they stop at regular intervals and celebrate with each other their accomplishments.

I believe that "work parties" are wonderful ways for people to be with one another, and if it is more fun to work with someone else than to work alone, people should take advantage of this!

Repeated trials compared with past performance

One type of "success" is exceeding one's own past performance by a significant amount. By this definition, EVERY student in a class can have frequent successes. It is one of the amazingly positive aspects of the human brain that with repeated trials of speed and accuracy (provided the student is working at the correct level on the hierarchy of difficulty), performance tends to improve, often very dramatically. Thus there is great opportunity for celebration and joy, when this is a frequent agenda.

By contrast, let's define the word "success" as meaning "being in the top 10% of one's class" or "being in the top 10% of students nationwide." Obviously, if we use this definition, 90% of students will be "failures." Furthermore, under this (or similar) definitions of success, education is a massive competition, where the better other people do, the worse you look.

This is not to say that group comparisons should not be done. It is useful to know where one stands relative to others. And competitions tend to bring out heights of human performance to some, as well as demoralization and a sense of failure to others. But the more the regular monitoring of student achievement can result in points plotted on the graph for that student, showing a positive slope, the more education becomes a joyous venture in which all can succeed and all can support each other's success.

Practice of touch typing and spelling

One of the most cherished skills that some of my students, and I, have picked up is the ability to think sentences and have the fingers automatically transfer them to print, without my having to think about which letter is where on the keyboard (or how to spell the words, or punctuate the sentences). It is possible that voice to text technology, aided by artificial intelligence, will become so refined that the skills of typing and spelling, and possibly those of grammar, will not be as useful to future generations. (If so, perhaps artificial intelligence can revise this book accordingly!) But for the present, this skill is one with a clear hierarchy of tasks, where practice has an effort-payoff connection, and where one person can be of clear help to another. It's a great one for older-peer tutoring.

When the skill of touch typing has reached a certain point, practice in it can be combined with practice in spelling. Words come onto the screen, and the learner simply copies it at the keyboard. When this task can be done accurately and fluently, the same batch of words is presented in about a one second flash apiece, and the learner types them from memory.

Practice of a fundamental writing task

So far in this chapter, I have emphasized practice as a means of picking up skills that can be perceived as somewhat tedious to acquire, and as a means of exercising self-discipline. (The goal is that these will be somewhat fun, not very tedious, to acquire if the activities are rigged correctly!) If education contains none of this, the student misses out on some very important skills, foremost among them the skill of tolerating repetitive practice. On the other hand, if education contains too high a fraction of this, the student misses out on creativity, invention, and higher order thinking skills versus committing things to declarative memory or muscle memory.

If I could revise my own education, one of the most fundamental changes would be the frequent assignment of the following writing task:

Please write something that you think is worthwhile for at least one other person to read.

Other than that, there are no restrictions: it can be prose or poetry, short or long, fiction or nonfiction. You can tell your own ideas or restate the ideas of others; if you do present other people's ideas, give them credit.

Depending on students' ages and skill levels, portions of classes, or entire class periods can be devoted to this task, perhaps with some discussion at the beginning in which students tell their intentions, and some discussion at the end in which they celebrate what they have accomplished and/or reflect otherwise on the experience. Another option is to leave time for students to read aloud to one another what they have written, and to discuss. A topic of discussion can be: what constitutes something that is "worthwhile" for someone to read?

Why is such a task not assigned more frequently? Part of the problem is that it is difficult to create a grading rubric for such an assignment. One of the major challenges of education is to design ways to disprove the following tenet: without the threat of bad grades hanging over their heads, students will have no other source of motivation.

Practice of a fundamental reading task

Here's another fundamental practice assignment:

During this class period, pick something that is worthwhile to read, and read it.

At the beginning of the period, students might discuss why they are choosing what they are choosing to read, and how they think reading it will accomplish something. At the end of the period, students might discuss what they found interesting or worthwhile about what they read.

Practice of a fundamental math task

The usefulness of the following class period presupposes that the students have been taught about the hierarchy of math skills and concepts. Where are they now? What do they need to have more practice in? What are the next skills on the hierarchy of difficulty that are reasonable to take on? Math students I have known are often totally clueless about what the overall game plan is for what topics and skills are on the agenda and how they fit together. Spending time studying, not just the next few assigned pages, but also the tables of contents, of well organized math textbooks can help. If teachers grasp the reason for presenting topics in a certain order, and can explain what those topics are and why they are in the order they are in, that helps enormously. With enough help, students can make good decisions in carrying out the following math assignment:

Make a decision based on where you are right now in your math learning, and do something during this time to advance that learning – to make progress.

As in the other exercises, goal-setting discussions can precede the independent activities, and celebration of accomplishments can follow them.

Doing these reading, writing, and math assignments help the student not just to learn the subject matter, but to learn the crucial skill of self-education. These all-purpose assignments are aimed at helping students not just to be compliant with what teachers assign them to do, but to self-assign, to be independent learners, to be goal-oriented in their education, to overcome the passivity that education sometimes induces.

Practice of psychological skills

No need to reinvent the wheel

Many people have looked upon skills such as emotional regulation, self-discipline, social conversation, conflict-resolution, and the like as something to be dealt with by "psychotherapy," which has different principles than those of education. It is true that the psychological skill realm carries its own special knowledge. But many of the principles of education generalize straight to psychological skills, without needed to be reinvented. Foremost among them is the principle that if we want someone to be expert at a certain psychological skill, we should help the person practice the *desirable* pattern of thought, feeling, and behavior, in the situation where the pattern will be used, to the criterion of fluency.

Practice in fantasy

The usefulness of fantasy rehearsal has been demonstrated in dozens of research studies. Accordingly, education should see as one of its major goals that positive patterns go through the neural pathways via imagination, often enough that they become thoroughly habitual.

Real life comes too fast for ideal practice

Why can't people simply wait to practice, for example, anger control or courage when they get into provoking situations? Because the situations of real life, particularly highly emotional ones, tend to demand fast responses. There is not time to deliberate about what the best response is. There is not time to practice at first haltingly, and then faster and faster. When a fast response is demanded in real life, people usually come out with the most practiced response in the repertoire, that is, what their current habit is. If they want to learn new habits, they need to practice without pressure. The ideal situation is a "psychological skills lesson," done when the person is not scared or angry, where the person can think carefully about the best response before practicing it. This is another reason why fantasy rehearsal with hypothetical situations is so important.

Psychological skills exercises.

If one wants to become expert at dancing, chess, basketball, golf, guitar, piano, public speaking, acting, touch typing, math computation, or any other skill, hardly anyone disputes that practice exercises are useful. The most accomplished people in each of these fields typically spend very large amounts of time in repetitive practice exercises.

When we think of mental health as a set of skills, we can use the same principle. We can practice those skills through psychological skills exercises. Let's examine some of them.

The celebrations exercise

This exercise is meant to help with the crucial task of generalizing all the psychological skills ideas to real life. It's also meant to exercise the skill of joyousness, particularly the ability to feel good about one's own positive choices. And finally, it is meant to provide social reinforcement for positive choices, when two people together celebrate the good things they've done. It's often done by two people: they take turns telling the other about something they are glad to have done – any time in their lives. Then they figure out which of the psychological skills (productivity, joyousness, kindness, etc.) the particular action was an example of. They might pay some attention to what the positive consequences were of their actions.

The twelve-thought exercise

The fundamental idea of cognitive therapy is that what we think plays a big role in determining our feelings and behaviors, and we can learn to notice and choose what to think, so as to make things turn out best for us.

The twelve-thought categorization helps to put this idea into an educational package. The twelve types of thoughts are:

1. Awfulizing. Recognizing the danger or harmfulness or loss in a situation. Example of not overdoing it: "My car won't start; this is frustrating; I don't like this." Example of overdoing it: "Everything turns out badly for me. There's no use trying to do things – something always messes it up."

2. Getting down on myself. Recognizing the undesirability of my own choice or skills. Example of not overdoing it: "I was rude to that person. I shouldn't have said what I did." Example of overdoing it: "I just can't get along with people; I'll never be worthy of someone having me as a friend."

3. Blaming someone else. Example of not overdoing it: "This person is trying to exploit me and not help me; I should be very careful about trusting this person." Example of overdoing it: "This _____ is just a total _____ idiot and

deserves to _____!!" (where the blanks are filled in with obscene or profane words and a horrible fate.)

4. Not awfulizing. A thought to the effect that the situation is not the end of the world, is capable of being handled. Example: "I may not like this, but I'll get through it and I'll be able to cope with it."

5. Not getting down on myself. A self-reminder not to be too self-punitive, even if one has made a mistake. Example: "I wasn't perfect on that, but it won't help things for me to beat myself up about it."

6. Not blaming someone else. A self-reminder that ruminating on the badness of the other person doesn't pay off past a certain point. Example: "That person may have done something I didn't like, but it won't help me to keep going over how badly they have behaved."

7. Goal-setting. Answering the question, what do I want to happen? Example: "My goal in this situation is to keep anyone from getting hurt and to stay out of trouble, and not to teach the other person a lesson."

8. Listing options and choosing. Example: "I could take the bus, get a ride with a friend, or walk. I think I'll walk today."

9. Learning from the experience. Example: I learned from this that if I want to do well on tests of this type, I need to start preparing lots earlier.

10. Celebrating luck. Example: Hooray, it's cool weather for my 10K race; that will make it much more pleasant!

11. Celebrating someone else's choice: I celebrate that someone over on the other side of the planet did a good job of making this guitar that I'm playing.

12. Celebrating my own choice: I give myself credit for doing lots of practice and getting myself really prepared for the concert I just put on.

For the twelve thought exercise, you choose any situation – positive, negative, or neutral. You make up an example of each of the 12 thoughts, pretending to be responding to that same situation. The point of this exercise is to build cognitive flexibility – to learn to respond to situations in any of these ways, whichever ways will help the most, rather than being stuck in habits. For example, people who are depressed tend to do a lot of getting down on themselves and not much celebrating of any sort. People with anger control problems tend to do a lot of awfulizing and blaming someone else. People with impulse control problems tend to give short shrift to goal-setting, listing options and choosing, and learning from the experience. By practicing all twelve, you get all of them into the repertoire, able to be chosen when helpful. To make this more of a social activity, two people can take turns with the thoughts – person 1 makes up an awfulizing thought, person 2 a getting down on self, person 1 blaming someone else, and so on.

The four-thought exercise

The four thoughts are a subset of the twelve thoughts. They are: not awfulizing, goal-setting, listing options and choosing, and celebrating your own choice. The idea of this exercise is to cultivate this sort of rational response as a default pattern when unwanted things happen. It sounds like this: "OK, I can handle this. Here's what I want to have happen.... I could do this, or that, or the other... I'll choose this. I think I did an OK job of choosing what to do." To make it social, people can use a list of situations and take turns, with person 1 doing all four thoughts with one situation, person 2 doing all four with the next situation, and so forth.

The divergent thinking exercise

Education, particularly testing, sometimes gives the mistaken impression that there is only one right answer to any question. But in decision-making, it's crucial to entertain more than one possible plan of action and to consider several possible consequences of the plan. And in creative thinking in general, it's crucial not to stop generating ideas once one has been generated. In overcoming impulsivity, it's crucial not to do the first thing that comes to mind, but to consider more than one possible action.

The divergent thinking exercise is meant to give a workout to the skill of coming up with several different ideas about a question. Someone wishes for something. What could the person wish for? Someone feels proud. What could the person have done that they feel proud about? Someone forgot something. What did they forget? The most fun way to do this is for two people to take turns generating possible answers. If the answers are whimsical or offbeat, that's fine; it's great to have fun with this.

The next two exercises, brainstorming options and pros and cons, are subsets of divergent thinking.

Brainstorming options

Research has shown that: 1) children who can generate more nonviolent options when given imaginary choice points tend to have better mental health; 2) option-generating is a teachable skill; 3) teaching option-generating tends to improve mental health. That would tend to imply that option-generating skill should be a part of education for all. (In reality, this skills is seldom systematically taught, either in schools or in therapists' offices.) To do the exercise, take any situation and practice giving lots of answers to the question, "What reasonable options should someone consider, in deciding what to do in this situation?" To make it a social activity, people can take turns generating options, and they can decide together which options they think are best after generating them.

Pros and cons

Once you've generated options, an important aid to decision making is to consider the advantages and disadvantages, or the pros and cons, or the good and bad consequences, of the option. To do the exercise, you take a situation and an option, and you generate as many pros and cons for that option as you can think of. People can take turns.

The reflections exercise

A reflection is a paraphrase of what you heard someone say, to make sure you understood it right, and to communicate that understanding to the other person. If after listening to someone else's utterance you start your response in one of the following ways, and fill in the blank, you're probably using a reflection.

So you're saying_____.

What I hear you saying is _____.

In other words, you're saying that_____.

If I understand you right, _____.

In the reflections exercise, one person talks (and stops talking frequently), and the other person does a reflection after each utterance. In a variation, one person makes up both parts of such a dialogue. In another variation, the person does reflections in response to written utterances.

Listening with four responses

If you are listening to someone else and do a reflection every time you open your mouth, you sound somewhat unusual. But you just sound like a good listener if you vary between reflections, facilitations, follow-up questions, and positive feedback. *Facilitations* is the term someone gave to utterances like uh-huh, I see, oh, yes, OK, and the like, which communicate, "I'm listening, you can keep going." Positive feedback can be statements like "That's interesting," "I'm glad you told me that," "Sounds like you made a good choice," etc. "Please tell me more about that," counts as a follow-up question, even though grammatically it isn't a question. To do the exercise, one person talks, and the other responds with whichever of the four responses seems most appropriate.

Tones of approval

You define three degrees of approval and enthusiasm in the tone of voice: neutral, small to moderate, and large. The differences largely depend on the pitch differences – neutral utterances tend to be monotone, and large approval and enthusiasm utterances tend to contain a big pitch range. One exercise is where person 1 gives examples of the different degrees, and person 2 guesses which one was meant. In another, person 1 specifies things to be said and the degree of approval, and person 2 tries to convey it – for example, "Can you say 'Yes, you got it,' with large approval?"

The social conversation role-play

Two people imagine that they are meeting somewhere, and that they are certain characters; they role-play an improvised social conversation. In a variation, one person makes up both parts, either by speaking them or by writing them.

Relaxation and biofeedback

The students learn about a given technique of relaxation: for example, tensing and relaxing muscles; relaxing muscles without first tensing; breathing 5 seconds in and 5 seconds out; saying a mantra to oneself such as the word *one*; visualizing relaxing and beautiful scenes; visualizing acts of kindness; doing the loving-kindness meditation. In the loving-kindness meditation, you refer to sentences such as:

May ____ become the best ___ can become.
May____ give and receive happiness.
May ____ live with compassion and peace.

The meditator wishes these things, first for the self, then one after another other person, and then perhaps groups of people.

In biofeedback, one uses a device to measure heart rate, fingertip temperature, skin conductance level for the fingertips, or heart rate variability, and notices the extent to which relaxation lowers heart rate, raises fingertip temperature, lowers skin conductance, and increases heart rate variability.

The conflict resolution role-play

This exercise is also known as the joint decision role play. (We're thankful that not all joint decisions turn into conflicts.) The two people imagine a joint decision or conflict of interests that two people are dealing with, and they role-play a conversation in which they meet each of the Dr. L.W. Aap criteria. Dr. L.W. Aap is a mnemonic for:

Defining: Each person defines the choice point from their point of view, speaking about their own needs and wishes and not blaming, accusing, or commanding the other.

Reflecting: Each person reflects the other's point of view to make sure they understand it correctly.

Listing: They list options for possible plans they could adopt.

Waiting: They wait until they finish listing before critiquing the options.

Advantages: They speak about the advantages and disadvantages of options (and not the bad aspects of the other person's personality).

Agreeing: They agree on some plan, even if it's just to continue thinking and table the decision to later.

Politeness: They do not raise the voice, interrupt, keep talking too long, or insult the other person.

A first step is teaching people to role-play imaginary conflicts with both of them meeting all 7 criteria for Dr. L.W. Aap. A more advanced skill is the ability to steer the conversation in the direction of meeting the criteria oneself, even when the other person is using more obstructive communications.

Skills stories

The student makes up a story in which someone does something wise or good. The student makes up a question for the reader, of the format: Was what the person

/ A. one psychological skill, or B. another? In ᵕ iation, the student sets out to make up a story exemplify᷈ᵤ᷈ a certain psychological skill; or in another, the student composes an example for each of the 16 skills, or several of the 62 skills.

Fantasy rehearsal

This is like a skills story, only the person composes the narrative as if it is happening to them in the present. The person rehearses handling a situation in just the way that they think best – not only with respect to behaviors, but also with respect to thoughts and emotions. One outline for fantasy rehearsals is STEBC: situation, thoughts, emotions, behaviors, and celebration. Written fantasy rehearsals can be especially useful, and can be read repeatedly as a way of practicing positive patterns.

The shaping game

There are two players: a shaper and a shapee. The shaper thinks of some behavior for the shapee to do, and writes it down (and perhaps draws a stick-figure picture): touch the wall, jump, sing a few notes, pick up the box of tissues, sit down and stand up 3 times, switch off and on the light switch, and so forth. The goal of both players is for the shapee to do the goal behavior. The only way the shaper can give clues is by congratulating the shapee on some behavior the shapee already did. So the shaper says things like, "I'm glad you're walking in that direction.... I'm glad you looked at the table.... I like it that you touched something on the table.... I like it that your hand got closer to the tissue box.... You did it! You picked up the tissue box!" This is meant to strengthen the use of positive reinforcement, both internally and in relations with others, and to help people become sensitive to the approving statements of self and others.

Individual decision making steps (SOIL ADDLE)

Someone imagines a choice point or picks one from a list. The person imagines what each of the following steps in decision making would sound like:
1. Situation. The person describes the situation, trying to include the aspects most relevant to the decision.
2. Objectives. What is the desired outcome? What am I trying to maximize or minimize?
3. Information. Let me look up or ask or otherwise find out information that will help.
4. Listing. Listing options
5. Advantages. Advantages and disadvantages of the most promising options.
6. Deciding. After weighing the advantages and disadvantages, making a choice.
7. Doing. Carrying out the choice.
8. Learning from experience. How did things turn out? Did I learn anything that will help with the next decision about a similar situation?

Practice and monitoring closely related

It would be desirable if we had well-standardized, normed measures for each of the exercises mentioned above, and more. But we can already roughly measure, over time, how well a student does at each of these exercises, over time. We can get the student to do most of these in writing, and we can compare the written work of the present to that of the past. We can do the essential activity that is analogous to that of runners watching their times gradually come down with increased effort: repeatedly practice and measure performance.

Skills exercises as writing assignments.

As I've mentioned several times, schools are under pressure to promote academic skill development, and this sometimes forms a reason not to work on psychological skills. Schools are expected to use scarce time resources to foster core academic skills, one of which is competent writing. But writing and psychological skills can be exercised simultaneously.

Here's an example of the celebrations exercise, posed in the form of a writing assignment:

Please write a narrative of a situation in which you did something you're glad you did. Clearly describe the situation you were in. Please recount your thoughts, your feelings, and your behaviors. What effects did your action have? Which psychological skill(s) is your action an example of? As you write this, please try to celebrate and feel good about your positive action!

Here's an example of the brainstorming options exercise, as a writing assignment.

The situation is that your sister has the flu. You want to be kind and supportive of your sister, but you don't want to catch the flu. Please list as many options as you can think of, for what you could do.

Here's a harder example, combining the brainstorming options exercise with pros and cons:

Please think of a choice point, where a person would do well to list options and choose. Please describe this situation in enough detail. Then please list at least 8 options for what the person could do in this situation. For the two options that you think are best, please list the advantages and disadvantages of those options. Then tell which option you would pick.

Here's an example of the social conversation role-play, posed as a writing assignment:

Someone sits next to someone on a bus or train. Please make up a conversation in which the two people have a pleasant conversation during the ride, and write out this dialogue. Please try to have each person follow as many of the guidelines about social conversation as you can remember.

With psychological skills exercises written out, the student gets a chance to practice both writing and the psychological skill in question. Plus, the teacher has a hard copy that can be compared to future performance, can be used as a measuring device, and can be used as a teaching device for other students.

Chapter 9: Reinforcement

Why should a student work on psychological skills? What's the payoff? Let's list a few:

1. Every psychological skill has its intrinsic payoff, in being able to handle life better. For example, the person who is good at social conversation enjoys social interaction more. The person who is good at self-discipline finds schoolwork more pleasant and less of a struggle.

2. If the student is convinced of the intrinsic worth of the psychological skill, (that is, if the efforts described in the chapter on goal-setting are successful) then there is an intrinsic payoff, a good feeling, in seeing oneself get better at it, independent of the life consequences. And good feelings are good for us!

3. If a teacher or preceptor is wanting and expecting the student to get better at the psychological skill, and the student has a positive relationship with that person, the student gets pleasure in pleasing that person.

4. If the person gets positive feedback on assignments that are done well, for example written versions of psychological skills exercises, the student may get pleasure from the approval.

5. If the student views measures of his or her performance over time, there is an intrinsic pleasure at seeing the performance get better and better.

But these sources of reinforcement may not be enough. One of the most challenging tasks of education is to create reinforcing consequences that will motivate even the students who for whatever reason do not possess a high degrees of "intrinsic" motivation.

The tones of approval exercise

I mentioned earlier the tones of approval and enthusiasm exercise as one to teach students. Like all the other exercises, this is very useful throughout the lifetime. Let's think about this as an exercise for teachers and for students who are tutoring other students.

Both teachers and student preceptors rely on verbal feedback for a good deal of their reinforcement of students. "That was a good job!" "You did it better than you've ever done it before!" "That's right!" These utterances are very important to most students.

These sentences were written with exclamation points. If they are spoken with exclamation points, they are much more reinforcing than if they are spoken with periods. There is something reinforcing on a very basic biological level about the ability to elicit an *emotional* response from another human being, not just a positive cognitive appraisal. I have witnessed over and over in work with children (as well as other human beings) that when the tone of voice of a tutor or teacher conveys emotion and enthusiasm, the motivation of the learner is sustained at a much higher level.

For many students, especially those called "stimulus-seekers," emotion from another person tends to be reinforcing, even when it is negative emotion. The moral is to speak excitedly when one wants to be reinforcing, and to speak quietly, slowly, and with more

144

monotone pitch when one wants to reprimand or correct or criticize.

As mentioned earlier, we can think of three degrees of approval and enthusiasm:

neutral
small to moderate approval
large approval

To practice the skill of regulating these tones: One person says things to the other, such as "That was a good job," or "You did it," or "Look at that," or "How are you today," or "You got them all right," with one of the three degrees of emotion and enthusiasm. The second guesses which one the first was trying to convey. Then they switch roles, and the second makes utterances and the first guesses. They do this to the criterion that correct guesses get made nearly all the time, and that both of them can do both small to moderate and large approval really well.

If teachers and tutors model more enthusiastic tones, they should notice: 1) more interest in the activity on the part of the students, and 2) more enthusiastic tones of voice emanating from the students. It's an interesting experiment for anyone to do! It's also interesting for anyone to try speaking to their own family members or friends with more approval and enthusiasm, and to see what the results are. Often the emotional climate of a relationship or a group can be improved by the unilateral action of one person.

The ranks and challenges system

Many years ago I worked at a summer camp and created a course in guitar-playing. The custom at this camp was that any instructors who wished could set up a system of ranks and challenges. Students who "passed a rank" by completing a requisite number of challenges would be recognized publicly: every so often there would be a "campfire" ritual in which all the campers filed into an outdoor amphitheater, watched a big pile of wood catch on fire, and sang some songs. Then the camp counselors who taught various courses would call those campers who had passed a rank, to receive their badges and be recognized. Campers would applaud each other's achievements.

I constructed a set of ranks and challenges for guitar playing, starting with the easiest challenges I could think of and moving up to the more complex ones – in other words, I constructed a hierarchy. I decided how many of these challenges was reasonable for a rank. I developed instructional techniques aimed specifically at each of the challenges. And I was gratified to see that as the campers gleefully passed my ranks and earned my badges, they learned to make very pleasant sounds come from their guitars.

This system was not at all foreign to me, because I had moved along a similar series of ranks in Boy Scouts – complete with catchy names for the ranks, badges, a place to wear the badges, and a social climate in which peers valued collecting the badges.

I noticed that the same system existed not only in every scouting organization, but also in nearly every martial arts training school – with belts of various colors replacing badges. As part of my camp work, I was asked to pass the rank of "Water Safety Instructor" within the Red Cross. I learned of a system of ranks and challenges for swimming as well: minnow, shark, sailfish, etc.

In some of these systems, students who have already passed a certain requirement are called upon to instruct another student in that requirement. When the more experienced student preceptor believes that the other student is ready to pass, the instructor is called upon for the final test. If the student passes, that is to the credit of both students.

Let's contrast the system of ranks and challenges – otherwise known as mastery learning – with the system usually used in schools:

For a typical course:

1. Time required from start to finish is fixed; each student goes from one challenge to the next at the same pace.
2. Proficiency gained varies (and is the basis for the grade).
3. Grades usually depend on performance relative to classmates, thus a competitive climate often prevails.
4. Students who need to move at a slower or faster pace tend to be frustrated or demoralized.

5. The motivations to get a good grade, and avoid a bad one, lead many students to work harder than they otherwise might.

For ranks and challenges, mastery learning:

1. The time required from start to finish is variable; each student goes at their own pace.
2. The goal is for all learners to become proficient.
3. The performance feedback is not, "Here's how you rank relative to peers," but "Congratulations, you passed the next level." Since the situation is not competitive, peers feel more like helping each other with the challenges.
4. Students who need to move at a faster or slower pace tend not to be frustrated or demoralized.
5. The chance to move along slowly without the penalty of a bad grade allows some students (for whom passing the next level is not reinforcing enough) to be lazy and coast along.

The ranks and challenges system is set up in order to maximally harness the social reinforcement of one's peer group. If the instructor can bring about the state that students consider it a strong status symbol to display the insignia of a higher rank, the problem of motivation and reinforcement is mostly solved. If the ceremonies in which awards are given are anticipated, experienced, and remembered with positive emotion, powerful reinforcement has been brought into play. If students can have daydreams about the time when they are called upon to be a mentor for a younger student and to successfully teach the student to do the challenges, more powerful reinforcement has been called into play.

These sources of motivation have been used successfully for decades by camps, scouting organizations, swimming teachers, and martial arts trainers. The mastery learning system appears relatively underutilized in schools.

My book entitled *Ranks and Challenges for Psychological Skills: Student Manual* describes a set of ranks and tells students how to achieve them. There is an accompanying tester manual for those who preside over seeing whether the student has passed a given level.

Other Awards

A school does not have to embrace totally the ranks and challenge approach and the mastery learning paradigm in order to make use of public recognition. What about having an assembly in which the students who have contributed ten or more positive models to the positive models bank since the last ceremony, to stand and be applauded? What about asking the students who have tripled their previous productivity time on one of the computer exercises, to stand and be applauded? What about publicly celebrating students who have worked on the editorial board for anthologies of psychological skills writings? Public recognition is a reinforcer that costs almost nothing and is limited only by the creativity of the staff.

Enlisting parents as "reinforcement officers"

Often, it appears that getting a phone call or an email from someone at a school is a very punishing event for a parent, because that communication is to let the parent know of some bad behavior of the student. I have heard many parents celebrate improvement in their children by proudly stating, "I don't get phone calls from the school any more."

Of course, when a parent gets a phone call stating that the child is acting badly or being lazy, most parents wish to "not just stand there, but do something," which usually takes the form of the parent's criticizing the child. Often it takes the form of the parent's nagging the child about homework assignments. Frustrated parents have described to me their relationship with their children as having devolved into a "battle royal" over school.

Let's imagine doing things differently. First, let's imagine that school staff convene parents, and explain to parents their crucial role in celebrating, with the child, the child's successes. The congregated mass of parents does the tones of approval exercise. (Large group practice of this can be a lot of fun!) Parents are taught other ways of reinforcing positive reports from school: with a bulletin board on which positive messages are displayed, with parades around the house, with special fun activities that only are done when the message from the school is positive, with special music that only gets played or sung at celebration times, with confetti, with announcements and applause around the dinner table, with the release of an electronic game that only comes out in celebration times,

150

and so forth. (When I was a homeschooling parent, one of the celebration mechanisms was a piggyback ride around the house, while participants belted out the melody of "The Stars and Stripes Forever.") If the parent's first words to the child upon seeing the child after school are excited celebration of some positive message from school, spoken in tones of large approval, the parent's role as "reinforcement officer" is fully engaged. If the parent communicates the child's accomplishment to someone else in the family, in the child's presence, and that person also celebrates the accomplishment, this is a big reinforcer, even if the child is not officially listening. To hear oneself spoken about in a positive way is quite reinforcing. I also recommend that parents have a celebrations time just before the child goes to bed, in which the parent mentions the child's positive behaviors as viewed by the parent, asks for the child's memories of positive behaviors, or celebrates the positive messages from the school.

How is it to be communicated to parents that a celebration is in order? In this age, the media most likely to succeed are probably text-messaging and email. The messages from teachers can be very short – teachers do not have time for detailed narratives. Certain code phrases can be adopted that will stand for longer narratives. Sometimes a simple rating of something on a scale of 10, with the message consisting of but a single number, is quite effective. Handing a piece of paper to a student, with hopes that the student will put in the backpack, remember to take it out, and get it to the parent is "so twentieth century."

Will most parents be able to celebrate as thoroughly and effectively as in this fantasy? "Many will be called and few will be chosen." But at least the school personnel will be encouraging parents to become the cheering section for the child rather than to be the punishers. And the net effect of that will surely not hurt anything, and may even help!

The positive models bank as reinforcer

In both the chapter on modeling and the chapter on goal-setting, I spoke of the positive models bank, a compendium of narratives of positive examples. One section of these can be positive models that students in the school have actually carried out, as witnessed by teachers. To have one's positive pattern dictated by a teacher and transcribed into a permanent record of positive models would be reinforcing for most students.

Who should do the transcription of teachers' dictations? (Or at least, the checking and revision of how dictation software puts them into text?) Hopefully, students. Such transcription falls solidly into the category of "useful work" that can be performed by students. Overseeing the rendering of narratives from dictation to print is an exercise in keyboarding, spelling, structuring sentences, punctuating, and various other academic skills. It is another example of work carried out not just to get a grade, but to do some good for someone.

Graphs as reinforcers

In the chapter on practice I spoke of keeping graphs of student performance on various tasks over time. I spoke of the wondrous nature of the brain, wherein if the same task is practiced repeatedly, the rate at which one can do correct performances of the task goes up significantly (provided that motivation is present and hierarchy-ology is attended to). The use of these graphs and their display can be very reinforcing. This is a form of reinforcement that we should not pass up if we can possibly get organized enough to take advantage of it. Again, teaching students to make graphs, whether by hand or computer program, is far superior to delegating this task to teachers.

Trips to the principal's office as reinforcers

In some schools, getting "sent to the principal's office" is used as a punishment. The poor principal, just as parents, is prevailed upon to chew out kids upon demand – a very unpleasant task for someone who went into the business because of a love of children. The principal or assistant principal or whoever, sometimes cultivates a stern, harsh, imposing demeanor which is judged successful to the extent that it creates fear motivation in students. Or sometimes the principal rebels against this role by being kind and loving and inadvertently reinforces kids for misbehavior.

Let's imagine an alternative scene wherein a student who outdid his or her own past record significantly enough, or who comes through with some outstanding model of fortitude or productivity or some such, is sent "to the office" where the principal can hear first hand from the teacher or from some other student what the student did. If the principal is not available, hopefully the principal's message-taker can be a substitute reinforcement officer, and take down the positive behavior and report it to the principal, who later stops by to reinforce the student.

Don't expend all reinforcers on sports

Like most things in life, the public recognition resources of a group are finite. We can't be applauding for each other all the time – we have to spend much of our time doing the things worth applauding for. In many schools, a great portion of the limited supplies of public recognition goes to athletic accomplishments. For example: if you walk into the main lobby of many high schools in this country, you will see an impressive collection of gold-colored metal in a trophy cabinet. These trophies celebrate the triumphs of the football team, the basketball team, the swimming team, etc., and occasionally the debate team or the chess team.

The competitive spirit is not something to be quashed. It is a reality of life, a reality of free enterprise business, and a reality of centuries of evolution that has been embedded into our genes. But – what if we used the competitive drive to reinforce more thoroughly the things that school really exists for: the teaching of academic and psychological skills that will be used throughout a lifetime? This contrasts, for example, with football skills, which are used by almost no students after schooling ends.

If a school is to have a trophy cabinet at all, how about using it to celebrate teams who improved the most in math or writing, the team that contributed most to the positive models bank; the team who produced the most improvement and love of learning through tutoring younger students; for the team which most exemplified psychological skills in real life?

Chapter 10: Instruction

Textbooks

In recent years textbooks seem to be disappearing. I've spoken to children who, for example, are very much confused about math, but who have no idea of where to turn if they want to read instructions, explanations, and examples. In times past, I would furnish an idea to students that was seemingly new to lots of them: before trying to do the problems, read how to do them in your textbook. And if you're behind, turn back to earlier pages in the textbook and read.

I remain convinced that it's extremely valuable to harness the countless hours spent by experts – time spent both in becoming expert in the first place, and in conveying that expertise through a well-organized and understandable textbook.

If we extend this reasoning to psychological skills: all children should have access to textbooks that explain how to be mentally healthy. But in the case of psychological skills, most people think of sending children to a counselor or therapist with the admonition of "You must talk!" without systematically teaching them anything.

This is not to say that talking with people about our problems is useless – it is often crucial. However, psychological skills constitute a corpus of information just like any other, that can be written down and studied.

The average person uses or needs at least one of the skills of emotional regulation, self-reinforcement, relaxation, joint decision-making, friendship-building, productivity, or self-discipline at least every waking hour. Why have human beings had textbooks of geometry at least since the days of Euclid, and have been without textbooks of psychological skills, in most schools, to this very day? Perhaps it's because not until very recently has the human race begun to employ the scientific method of determining what is psychologically healthy. In the 1960's and 1970's, serious scholars suggested that breaking things or pounding on things or screaming might be a harmless way of "releasing aggression." This idea was called the "catharsis hypothesis." In the latter part of the 20th century, however, numerous experiments taught us that attempts to "release aggression" usually enhanced aggressive urges rather than diminishing them. These experiments are landmark efforts to determine whether strategies of dealing with life situations "work" or not. Similarly, in the latter part of the 20th century the study of psychotherapy began to become "manualized": that is, experimenters would write the content of the psychotherapy into a manual so that it could be replicated by other investigators. Accordingly, we began to be able to test empirically whether giving certain messages to people helped them or not. We found out, for example, that when people have unrealistic fears, it helps a lot to ask them to arrange the feared situations in order of how scary they are, and to go from least scary to most scary in practicing desirable ways of handling those situations. We found that it does not help as much to ask them to remember their dreams and try to figure out what they mean.

Often the manuals used in mental health are directed toward the practitioner or the instructor, who reads the manuals and then makes up the words by which the content will be delivered to the client or student. It is much more direct for experts to speak directly to the student. This, of course, is what is done in the "psychological self-help" genre of books. But such books have not been used very much in the service of mental health for children.

Much of my own career has been spent in writing and using textbooks of psychological skills for students. Perhaps I can be forgiven for emphasizing my own books, by my being subject to the "availability heuristic": spending time writing a psychological skills curriculum does tend to make the books one has written more noticeable. In the spirit of availability, these are available, at no cost, to anyone with an Internet connection, at josephstrayhornmd.com. The following is a description of some of them.

Illustrated Stories that Model Psychological Skills

For preschoolers through early grade schoolers, these are a set of illustrated stories that are meant to exemplify productivity, joyousness, kindness, etc.

Plays that Model Psychological Skills

These are plays meant to be performed for and with young children, with toy people, as an introduction to the important skill of dramatic play, and as models of each of the psychological skills. Also, they can be read aloud by beginning readers in collaboration with a tutor.

The Letter Stories

These are a set of illustrated stories in which the main characters are letters of the alphabet, with arms and legs and faces. They do helpful things to people by saying their phonetic sounds and blending them together to say just the word that people need to hear. The child hearing these is exposed to the ideas that each letter makes a sound and that blending sounds together makes words. They also may learn to sound and blend a number of words useful to the beginning reader.

Manual for Tutors and Teachers of Reading

This book explains how to teach reading. The tutor or teacher is taught how to assess and teach phonemic awareness, spatial awareness, and letter-sound correspondence, the foundation skills of reading. When the foundation skills are in place, there is a hierarchical series of word lists for practice in "sounding and blending," such that the words in any given list have the same phonetic principle. The drills and exercises are meant to simultaneously build self-discipline, and the stories for reading practice are meant to simultaneously model psychological skills. Much of the manual has to do with the interpersonal skills needed by tutors.

If psychological skills are the set that help one to be happy and to make others happy, reading certainly qualifies as a psychological skill. The children who are compelled to attend school but who can't read well enough to understand what they are asked to do tend to be a miserable bunch, and helping them to become experts at reading can change their life trajectories.

Programmed Readings for Psychological Skills

This is an introductory textbook of psychological skills. The student gets many models of the sixteen skills and principles, the twelve types of thoughts, the principles of fear reduction, ways of listening to another person, the principles of conflict-resolution, the 62 skills, and other concepts.

A Programmed Course in Friendship-Building and Social Skills

This gives tips on how to use greeting and parting rituals, figure out what to say in social conversation, be a good listener, participate in games, have a good sense of humor, keep your cool rather than losing your temper, and other ideas.

A Programmed Course in Self-Discipline

This covers topics of setting goals, forming an "internal sales pitch" to motivate oneself toward goals, making a plan for goal-attainment, identifying the most important choice points, using fantasy rehearsals, using self-monitoring and self reinforcement, continuing to read about how to carry out the goal, using "advanced self discipline" to learn to enjoy the work toward the goal, and other ideas.

A Programmed Course in Conflict-Resolution and Anger Control

This describes what rationality is, and why rational response to provocation and conflict is the goal rather than letting one's own hostility out. It provides menus for choosing one's thoughts, emotions, and behaviors in response to provocation and conflict. It advocates nonviolent sources of power, and promoting a positive emotional climate.

Reading About Math

Math students often spend much more time struggling to solve problems than reading to understand the principles behind solving them. This book, by contrast, is nothing but explanation, with a comprehension probe every 200 words or so, in the same programmed format as several of the other books. It is designed to present math as a reading comprehension activity.

Math is not usually considered a psychological skill, but the cure and prevention of "math anxiety" or "math avoidance" or "math demoralization" can result in great improvement in mental health.

Learning Math Facts with the Broken Number Line

This is a way of teaching the basic facts of addition, subtraction, multiplication, and division, using "broken number lines" to make practice more pleasant for the student.

A Programmed Course in Anxiety Reduction and Courage Skills

This covers the principles and methods of reducing unrealistic fears and aversions.

Exercises for Psychological Skills

This explains not just the exercises presented earlier, but some 60 exercises, explained and modeled.

A Programmed Course in Psychological Skills Exercises

This explains why and how to do psychological skills exercises; it's in programmed format, with an A or B multiple choice comprehension probe every couple of hundred words or so.

Instructions on Psychological Skills

An explanation of how and why to do each of the 62 psychological skills. This is a fairly big book, but I've found that it lends itself to a reader's opening it to a random page and picking a random paragraph; often the paragraph will contain some useful thought about how to be mentally healthy. Reading and re-reading it from start to finish is also welcomed, for those with adequate productivity skills for this task.

The Competence Approach to Parenting, A Programmed Course for Parents, and *Reinforcement and Punishment.*

These are about how to be a good parent. It would appear sensible for people to study this subject before becoming parents rather than after, for example in high schools. Even for those who wish never to become parents, the principles of human relations will not be lost upon them.

Ranks and Challenges for Psychological Skills: Student Booklet, and *Tester's Booklet*

These designate the requirements for levels of psychological skill expertise, and explain to the reader how to meet these requirements. These represent a mastery learning approach to psychological skills exercises.

Manual On Task-Switching or Set-Shifting

There are several activities that require a person to respond to similar stimuli repeatedly, but with different directions applied. For example, you see the word blue printed in red. The directions at times may be, "What is the word," and at other times, "What color is the word?" It's fairly well established that on the average, people with ADHD have trouble with such tasks, that the brain regions in charge of such tasks are also involved in other "executive functions," and that practice can lead to improvement in task-switching. Whether sustained practice generalizes to other executive functions is in question. This manual hedges its bets by presenting a bunch of academic tasks for task-switching. Even if there is not generalization,

163

the tasks such as math facts, math word problems, and word recognition are useful to practice anyway.

Pictures, Words, and Numbers

This book is intended to teach the mathematics of page-finding. The page numbers of a book provide a useful analogue to a number line. This book provides a colored photograph on each page, with a label for the object pictured, and a big prominent page number at the bottom of the page. It lends itself to exercises on finding numbered pages.

Psychological Skills Questions on Novels

The programmed manuals provide many questions that build proficiency in linking concrete behaviors or utterances to psychological skills concepts. For example, when someone did this behavior, what psychological skill was that an example of? When someone thought this, which of the 12 thoughts was it? When someone said that, which of the ways of listening was it? This manual provides similar questions regarding the thoughts, feelings, and behaviors of characters in trade books that are probably more entertaining than much of the material in straight psychoeducational writing. Some *Boxcar Children* books, *Mrs. Frisby and the Rats of NIMH,* and several others have been "skillized."

Big Ideas To Ponder and To Use

Of the ideas that people come across in the course of "becoming educated," which are the ones that help us the most? Which are most important to understand? This book is my attempt to answer that question, with a brief explanation of lots of ideas.

Psychoeducational Tutoring

This is a book explaining the rationale of psychoeducational tutoring, research findings giving evidence for its various components, and some detailed directions on how to provide it.

The programmed format

B.F. Skinner was one of the pioneers of "programmed instruction." Skinner hoped that by breaking learning down into small units, asking for responses frequently from the learner, and having those responses reinforced, learning could be dramatically improved.

For a time, "programmed instruction" was in vogue. Books were produced in the format Skinner had pioneered – in small frames. The reader would be asked a question on one page, and would turn the page to see the answer, plus the next question, in the frame on the next page.

Programmed instruction has now been incorporated into computerized instruction. But it hasn't revolutionized education as much as Skinner hoped it would. Perhaps one problem is that computers' responses to right answers are not as potent reinforcers as one might hope. However, the principles of keeping the learner engaged in answering questions rather than simply passively taking in the reading, and of breaking down the material into units small enough to be tested by one question, makes sound educational sense.

In the programmed books I've written, the format is a different from that of the traditional programmed book. The reading passages are longer than in the traditional programmed book, so that the reader is taking in organized units of information, rather than bit by individual bit. The answers to the questions are not on the next page, and indeed they are usually nowhere in the book.

Whence, then, comes the reinforcement for correct answers of the questions? From another human being – social reinforcement. The tutor says, "I think you're right!" "I agree!"

There is also a computerized version of the programmed manuals, the "readask" program, where the computer does provide feedback. But this is much more effective when the student does it with a human preceptor who gets excited over correct answers.

Taking in instruction as a social activity

Reading books is an amazingly efficient way to take in information; writing books is a very efficient way to transmit it. One of the main problems, however, is that students are hungry for interaction with other human beings, and sitting by themselves studying a book does not serve that function. For this reason, many students would prefer to poke each other or grab possessions away from each other rather than sit silently and study. Even though the former activities seem pointless and senseless, they are motivated by the hunger for interaction: for alternately affecting and being affected by someone else.

In the psychoeducational tutoring model I have experimented with, I have given books with no illustrations, mostly without gripping plots, around 100,000 words long, to children in early grade school, and have had them read every word from start to finish. How does this happen? By pairing the young person with an older tutor, who makes the reading of the book a social activity.

The book is divided into sections of about 200 words, and after each section there is a comprehension question. They take turns reading the sections – e.g. the tutor reads the odd numbered ones, and the student reads the even numbered ones. The student answers each comprehension question, and the tutor either agrees or states what the correct answer is. If either wants to discuss the readings at any point, they are free to discuss with each other.

The alternate reading format can be done between a tutor and a student, or between peer and peer. This format turns a solitary activity into a social activity.

Instruction as comprehension practice

Every major general achievement test, including third grade achievement tests, college admission tests, and tests for admission to graduate school or medical school, test reading comprehension. Each does it in much the same way: by presenting passages of written paragraphs and asking questions about them. Indeed, this widespread practice makes sense, because the ability to read and understand the written word is one of the primary skills of an educated person.

The programmed format also gives much opportunity for practice in reading comprehension tests – and more importantly, in reading comprehension itself.

There's another way that the programmed instructions I've written can be used in schools: the students simply read a good number of sections and write down the answers, after which the answers are checked. Then they go back and learn from their mistakes. In other words, the students practice a reading comprehension test.

In a hybrid between the social model and the reading comprehension test model, two peers work together, alternately reading each section aloud and answering the question. They arrive at the answers by consensus and then their answers are checked.

Instruction written to the student

Many curricula are written to the teacher – here is what you are supposed to say; ask the students this; and so forth. In the programmed instructional books, the curricula are written directly to the student, who ideally reads them while taking turns with a tutor. This is not a revolutionary idea, but it is an important distinction to be aware of when thinking about curricula.

Benefits of reading aloud

Even for middle and high school students, and even for adults, reading aloud has great benefits. First, many students retain sloppy reading habits of ignoring certain words, misreading certain words for others, and making random errors. Lots of silent reading can sometimes only more thoroughly practice bad habits. Reading aloud provides auditory feedback about these errors. When you hear yourself, it occurs to you to correct yourself and get it right. You begin the sort of practice that promotes steps toward mastery. Second, reading aloud allows the student to reveal the results of the complex judgments of what sort of emotional tone the passage should be read with. In reading aloud, the constant decision making about what tones should be used probably engage an important part of the brain that can lie dormant when one is taking in words spoken tonelessly in inner speech. Third, the art of fluent oral language is a very important psychological and interpersonal skill, and reading fluently is a very good way of practicing this. Just getting coherent words from the brain to the mouth, whether composed by someone else or by oneself, is important practice. And fourth, the art of clear speech is another important skill that can be practiced by reading aloud. Finally, as noted before, reading aloud renders the written word a social activity as opposed to a solitary one. For all these reasons, lots of time spent with students taking turns reading aloud to each other is a major part of the vision of schools that teach psychological skills.

Chapter 11: Stimulus Control

Punishment versus stimulus control

Imagine that someone is trying to help a child with homework, at the kitchen table; another family member is watching television in the kitchen, and other family members come in an out to get something to eat. The homework-doer fails to pay close attention, speaking to other family members and fixating on the television often.

Human beings often have an urge to punish when others don't cooperate. The homework-helper may have the urge to reprimand the homework-doer, or to take away a privilege, or to slap him into submission.

But none of these interventions would be as likely to work as well as stimulus control. Stimulus control means arranging the environment so that the stimuli in it tend to elicit the desired behavior. That is: certain stimuli are either hard-wired or conditioned to elicit certain responses. If the homework-helper wants better attention, the first choice intervention is to move the work site, if possible, to an environment where distractions are minimal. Doing this can obviate the question of whether to punish inattention.

As another example of stimulus control: anyone who has tried to lose weight will know that if brownies, potato chips, cookies, and all other sorts of tasty high-caloric foods are left within sight and within reach, the difficulty in resisting them is great. If very tempting foods are not even present in the house, it is much easier to avoid them.

The magic of one-on-one

A study I published examined the behavior of children in individual tutoring as contrasted to their behavior in classrooms. The improvement in behaviors characteristic of attention deficit hyperactivity disorder, in the one-to-one situation, was large – as big as that achieved by medication. Why should this be so? Because in well-conducted individual tutoring, the student can at any given instant be receiving feedback from the tutor or anticipating feedback momentarily. The student does not need to tolerate sitting unnoticed while other people are getting attention. In addition, peers who have become associated with conflict or stimulus-seeking annoyance are not temptingly present. The overall noise level is usually much less. And finally, hierarchy-ology is on the side of the one-on-one situation, because the student can be challenged at just the level that is appropriate for that student.

The stimulus of skillfully-behaving others

If there is a stimulus that as powerfully elicits productivity as one-to-one work, it is being in a whole group of people, all of whom are being intently productive. In such circumstances, the natural tendency for human beings to conform to the prevailing behavior of their social group kicks in, in the service of productivity. If very positive group norms get started, there is an influence on each group member to sustain them. Of course, the problem for the educator is how to set up such group norms in the first place. I have heard of the strategy of starting with pairs of workers, and gradually adding to the size of the group, such that each person who is added to the group is subject to the positive norms already established. This is not an option for the typical classroom teacher, who is delivered a prefabricated group that may or may not have positive norms already established.

What I say about groups with norms of productivity also applies to other psychological skills: joyousness, kindness, honesty, and so forth.

One option that probably has not been harnessed fully enough in education is for groups of children to pay conscious attention to the norms that they are setting for each other. My guess is that most students do not think much about how the behaviors they display elicit positive or negative behaviors from others. Perhaps by paying more attention to social climates, it may be possible for students to take more responsibility for shaping them in desirable ways.

Exercise, and the stimuli that elicit it

Millions of students, particularly boys, exhibit problems of restlessness, fidgetiness, and too high an activity level in school. Meanwhile, in many schools recess is short, and some days have no gym class. Whereas several decades ago, students would have walked a mile or more to school, today fear of kidnapping and traffic accidents have all but eliminated self-propelled

172

transportation. We are often asking children to go without significant exercise throughout the entire school day.

This pattern is in marked contrast to the pattern of our prehistoric ancestors, and most of our ancestors throughout recorded history. Life during most of human evolution probably consisted of constant foraging for food, involving moving around during most waking hours. After the agricultural revolution, exercise spent in hunting and gathering was replaced by exercise in farm work, but it was a huge amount of exercise nonetheless.

The expectation that children would spend long days sitting and working at desks is a very recent invention in human history. The human body certainly did not evolve in such circumstances.

I believe that a large fraction of stimulus-seeking misbehavior, restless misbehavior, and irritable misbehavior of children would be eliminated or reduced if schools would return to the quantities of physical exertion that the human body was meant for.

What are the stimuli that promote exercise in children? The answers are almost infinite. The most time tested option is simply to turn the children loose with space to run. If we want to throw money at the problem, we purchase a bunch of fancy exercise machines, such as stair steppers or elliptical trainers or treadmills or stationary bikes, each of which is complete with a place where a video may be viewed. We schedule each child with ample time each day with a very educational video to watch while the child uses the machine. (Actually, if we choose non-motorized treadmills and used audio or video players, this option is not so terribly expensive.)

For those schools where it is possible to go outside and walk without incurring the danger of being killed either by a vehicle or another human being, taking hikes or runs is a great option. When there is any indoor space, running around it or back and forth across it is a great option. Competitive sports are an obvious solution. Not so obvious is cooperative sports – I'll say more about this later. Having everyone in the class take a five minute organized calisthenic break is another option, where the teacher takes on a second career as a fitness coach or aerobic dance instructor. A less structured option is one where students are asked to independently figure out how to burn as much energy as possible in the five minutes, by jumping up and down, running in place, doing exercises of their own choosing, dancing, or whatever. With an inexpensive quantity of rope, the fine art of rope-jumping can be taught as part of the school curriculum. This is an art that has been honed to a great degree of proficiency by some inner city children. Another option is including dance as part of the curriculum for all students. In this option, students by the end of their education would have learned all the major steps of ballroom dance, various modern dance moves, an introduction to tap dancing, square dancing, clogging, or whatever else can be taught. Throughout the day, for example, the teacher would call for an exercise break, put on a cha-cha or mambo or samba song, and let the students do the steps on their own, right beside their desks. Pedometers may be used to monitor steps. If one searches the Internet for "bodyweight exercises," a whole panoply of no-equipment exercises have been devised. I have experimented with strength-building exercises that require no weights, where one hand pushes or pulls with the other hand supplying the resistance, which can be done at the same time as squats.

A great game for exercising is "follow the leader." Someone (at first the teacher, later rotating among students) is the leader; that person does different physical movements, dance or otherwise, in time with music or otherwise. The followers mimic the leader's movements. It's a simple game, but it can be much fun and great exercise.

Periodic measurement of fitness levels is an activity worth including. These can be done by running a certain distance or by a variety of step tests with measurement of heart rate, or by many other means. If the students are doing enough exercise to get progressively fitter and fitter, they may be getting enough to help them be less restless and fidgety and to be able to relax successfully into seated academic work.

Finally: another major stimulus to exercise is the taking on of *useful work* tasks that involve physical labor. Does there seem to be something strange about the picture when people drive to gyms, and run on electronic treadmills, while other people use gas powered snowblowers to remove the snow from the sidewalk? Does there seem to be something incongruous when students are kept sitting in classrooms, being taught in health class about the value of exercise, being distracted by the noise of gas mowers cutting the grass outside their windows? I'll speak more about this topic in the chapter on *useful work*.

Electronic distractors

Now for an important aspect of stimulus control, as of the current era: electronic amusement. We are living in a world where the experience of childhood has been completely transformed by cell phones, videogames, social media, and other electronic entertainment. Informal sports have been displaced by networking through videogames. Social conversation has been displaced by people gazing at their cell phones rather than looking at or speaking with each other. Reading books has been displaced by reading a few sentences on hyperlinked electronic pages, and then going on to the next link. Writing letters has been displaced by terse text messages. Texting in many cases replaces actual oral conversation. And the content of videogames is very much skewed toward violence, with opportunities for thousands of virtual violent acts within a very short time.

If one wants to allow students to focus on the activities outlined in this book, stimulus control is necessary. Free access to the Internet and all its temptations, as well as the temptations loaded onto most cell phones, has to be limited.

One of the problems with using stimulus control is that the computer is an integral part of modern life and can be a tremendously useful tool for education. How to make the desired tools available while restricting access to the undesirable temptations is in itself a technological challenge that appears to be soluble with expert programming, although the expertise at undermining any restrictions will grow to oppose it.

The ultimate goal of stimulus control strategies is a progression to the point where people do not have to be controlled by the efforts of other people, but can use a combination of self-discipline and self-imposed stimulus control to avoid temptations. The ideal school might help students progress through a series of stages, for example the following.

1. Access to tempting electronic amusement and communication is simply not present.

2. Access to certain nonviolent electronic amusement is presented as a reinforcer for accomplishments requiring self-discipline. Access is still totally controlled by school staff.

3. Students use computers for academic tasks; these have access to unwanted distractors technologically disabled.

4. Students use computers for academic tasks where access to unwanted distractors is not disabled, but there is periodic monitoring of whether the student is able to avoid the distractors.

5. Students are taught, in formal coursework, exercises, discussion, etc. about the challenge of electronic distraction. They are taught about activities that are

alternatives to electronic amusement. They are challenged to form their own goals for avoiding distraction in the electronic world they exist in.

6. Access to devices is gradually increased, and students continue to think, write, and speak about their goals of avoiding tempting distractors, to monitor their success in avoiding them, use nonviolent amusement as reinforcement for self-discipline tasks, and to help each other with this important life skill.

7. As in adult life, students have full access to devices, but are expected to use good judgment in avoiding distracting themselves and others. (This is an expectation that many adults currently do not fulfill.)

In other words: the challenge of dealing with electronic distraction in modern life is treated as one that is applicable to all students, and conscious attention is paid to this challenge throughout education. Educators endeavor not to be satisfied with imposing rules upon the unwilling, but strive to help motivate their students to set their own goals for reasonable coping with the world of screens.

Chapter 12: Monitoring

In this chapter are some ideas about monitoring, or measurement, of the outcomes we wish to promote.

That which is measured gets improved

If it is very important for us to improve something, then we usually should measure it very frequently. Why is there such a relationship between measurement and improvement? Because frequent monitoring keeps people focused on the goal. It reminds people of what they are trying to achieve. It tells us when we are not achieving progress, and allows us to problem-solve in this circumstance, and change course if necessary to resume progress. It provides the opportunity for reinforcement and celebration of progress. Without monitoring, the student does not realize when he has "set a new record" for himself.

Things that are harder to measure

It is easy to measure which of two athletic teams has the better performance on a given day – we simply have them play football, have them race in swimming or track, or whatever, and the usual rules quantify the score. Over the course of a season, a great number of individual and team statistics are accumulated. This is part of what makes sports fun.

It is also fairly easy to measure reading recognition, reading comprehension, and mathematics skills. Standardized tests and teacher-constructed tests can do a reasonably reliable and valid job of this. Writing skills are somewhat more challenging to measure, because they usually involve the subjective judgment of a trained human being. Still, asking someone to write something and scoring the result in some standard way gives a decent measurement.

When we get to psychological skills, however, the measurement task is more difficult. How do we measure how self-disciplined someone is, or how kind, or how joyous? There are a variety of techniques, but they don't always agree with each other. They don't always agree with repeat performances of themselves. Sometimes people act much different in different settings – which one is the "real thing?" For example, a child appears self-controlled at school, but has lots of major tantrums at home. The teachers and parents have very different ideas about the child's fortitude skills, not because they are bad raters, but because the child actually behaves with more fortitude at school. Or a child appears very kind when the teacher is looking, but bullies others behind the teacher's back.

Despite the fact that psychological skills are in general more difficult to measure than athletic and academic skills, we nonetheless should attempt to measure them, because they are so important. At times, teachers have come under tremendous pressure to improve standardized test performance in their students. Reading comprehension, math, and writing skills are very important, and it is in many ways good that tests monitor these skills. But psychological skills are even more important. If a child learns to solve equations but substance addiction precludes their using math skills, what good has the math work accomplished? If a student scores high on all standardized tests, but goes on violent destructive rampages, the academic achievement is for naught.

Rating scales

A reasonable approximation to measurement is to ask someone who observes the person often (including, possibly, the person himself) to rate the person's behavior and skill with a Likert scale: does the person do this behavior very often, often, sometimes, or never? Is the person highly skilled, fairly skilled, not very skilled, or very unskilled? On a scale of 0 to 10, how much fortitude does this person show? We get more reliable measurements from these scales when several items are added or averaged.

A major advantage of these scales is that they are quick. One can obtain a rating in a matter of minutes. Another advantage is that they can reflect the knowledge gained in many hours, days, or months of observation, whereas any one performance test is a sample of a few minutes or at most a few hours of the person's behavior. And rating scales tend to ground us in real life. For example, suppose a neuropsychological test based on making correct responses to images flashed onto a computer screen shows that a student is getting better and better at "executive functioning." This is celebration-worthy, but if teachers, parents, and the student himself report no change on ratings of everyday behavior, it appears that improvement has not generalized. For this reason, we need rating scales.

Despite their necessity, rating scales will always be fairly crude and imprecise. What is the difference between scale descriptors of "often" and "sometimes?" And how is a rater supposed to average out the behavior of students whose behavior varies widely over time? What if we were to give track runners trophies according to observers' ratings on rating scales where they were marked as running extremely fast, very fast, sort of fast, not too fast, and really slow? What if, instead of SAT and ACT tests or IQ tests, we substituted people's ratings of the person as "very smart," "fairly smart," and so forth? We'd lose a great deal of precision in our measurement.

Yet, teachers who have filled out recommendations of students to college and graduate school know that despite testing, college admission officers still want the gut feelings of teachers as assessed by rating scales. The "Common Application Teacher Evaluation" includes items like this: "Compared to other students in his or her class year, how do you rate this student in terms of: academic achievement: below average, average, good (above average), very good (well above average), excellent (top 10%), outstanding (top 5%), one of the top few encountered in my career." Another item is "intellectual promise." Thus despite all our technology in testing, we still find it useful to ask questions synonymous with "Please rate how smart this student is."

While speaking about the Common Application: The Likert scale therein is used not only for academic

182

achievement, but for psychological skills. The phrase from the Common Application is in quotations, while the phrase from the 16 skills and principles that I would regard as synonymous is in parentheses after:

"disciplined work habits" (productivity, self-discipline)
"integrity" (honesty)
"reaction to setbacks" (fortitude)
 "concern for others" (kindness, respectful talk)
"initiative, independence" (aspects of productivity and courage)
"self-confidence" (combination of courage and joyousness)

Direct observational counts

A gold standard for behavioral research has been to hire observers, work out very carefully what the definition of a certain behavior is, and have those observers focus complete attention upon a person, counting each instance of the defined behaviors. For example: of the total number of times a student is issued a directive by a teacher, how many complies are there, how many ignores, and how many defies?

Some researchers or clinicians have asked parents or teachers to do behavior counts. In many years of practice, I have never seen a parent or teacher who could sustain the effort of counting behavior over weeks or months, in addition to their usual duties. Direct observational counts require too much labor and effort and organization.

Sufficient observation is necessary

In self-contained classrooms where the same teacher observes a student throughout the school day, ratings are probably most valid. In middle schools and high schools where any one teacher gets a smaller exposure to a student each day, ratings are often more problematic. And in all these settings, the rating of social behavior is often difficult: bus rides and lunchtimes sometimes provide the best sample of social behavior, during which time no one is observing the student very closely except peers.

Rating and feedback as intervention

Just as when in games, players usually try harder when they decide to keep score, students will often greatly improve their behavior when they know that someone is measuring it. This is especially true when the behavior ratings are recorded and displayed by a parent, as on a graph or table. I've seen substantial improvements in children's behavior when a teacher simply assigns one global Likert rating to the student's behavior each day: how well did the student do, on a scale of 0 to 10? If the student has a score to shoot for, even when the score is tied to no reinforcers other than the interest and approval of the parent and teacher, the child can be very favorably motivated. Similarly, children can be strongly motivated by receiving a global rating from the parent regarding the child's behavior during the time with the parent.

Ratings can be linked to contingent reinforcers

If the things the student wants – physical possessions, access to entertainment, privileges – are made contingent upon the student's performance on the ratings, there is now extrinsic motivation in addition to the motivation of just seeing how well one can do. Researchers have debated how much the giving of extrinsic motivation may weaken intrinsic motivation. This argument tends to become moot in the case of students who clearly lack the intrinsic motivation to get the job done, and the job is crucial to do.

My guess is that any weakening of intrinsic motivation is less of a problem in programs that run loosely rather than tightly. Tight programs involve a specific contract, for example: you will get this prize on the very day that you collect a moving average of this rating over this number of days. Then, when the student collects the prize, the motivation can be expected to go down until the next one is offered. On the other hand, here's an example of a loose program: A parent simply keeps a child's daily ratings on display, and then, when the child asks for some discretionary reinforcer, the parent walks to the chart, deliberates, and decides on the basis of how the behavior has been lately. There is still a contingent relationship between behavior and reinforcement, but it is now not so tight that one can expect motivation to go down when the prize is delivered.

Making the child's most desired reinforcers contingent on psychologically skillful behavior is a powerful intervention. However, it's not one to be undertaken lightly. If parents or teachers undertake such a program, they should be prepared to continue it for at least a year. Moving from a "paid employee" to a "volunteer worker," especially without having been consulted about that change in status, often leaves the child feeling as rebellious as an adult employee might feel.

The Psychological Skills Inventory

If psychological skills are what we are interested in increasing, it makes sense to rate them directly. In appendices to this book are three versions of psychological skills inventories that I have used. The items tend to be correlated with one another fairly highly, and they sum to form a global measure of psychological health. These are simply ratings of productivity, joyousness, kindness, honesty, fortitude, and so forth, i.e. the psychological skills mentioned throughout this book.

Exercises can be measures

Performance measures of psychological skills have some advantages over rating scales. Just as performance tests can be made into skill development exercises, skill development exercises can be made into performance tests. For example:

The celebrations exercise. Asking a person to recount the positive examples of psychological skills that the person has done recently, and counting the number of positive examples that can be recalled, is likely to be a measure that would correlate with the person's morale, confidence, achievement, and positive mood.

The four-thought and twelve-thought exercises. You give the individual standard situations, and ask him or her to write an example of each of the four thoughts or the twelve thoughts in response to that situation.

Brainstorming options. You give the individual standard hypothetical situations, and ask the person to generate as many reasonable and good options as possible in a certain time. The options the person generates are compared to a standard list prepared for that situation. Each option on the standard list that the person has mentioned adds one to the score. This procedure eliminates much of the subjectivity from the scoring procedure.

Pros and cons: You give the individual hypothetical actions, and ask the person to generate pros and cons for that action. One point is given for each of the advantages or disadvantages the person mentions that is also on a standard list.

Reflections, rated version: The person is given utterances, and composes reflections responsive to those utterances. Raters holistically rate the empathy and appropriateness of the reflection.

Reflections, multiple choice version: The person is given an utterance and several possible reflections; the person picks the one that is most empathic and accurate.

Tones of approval. The person is given several utterances to say with specified tones of approval; the utterances are scored as to whether they agree with the tones specified.

The social conversation role-play. The student, given a setting and a description of characters, composes a social conversation between the two, in writing. This is scored according to criteria for a positive social conversation. This may be spoken or written by the student.

Social conversation in real life. The student participates in a standard interview, in which the student is to have as pleasant and meaningful as possible social conversation with the interviewer.

Relaxation and biofeedback. How much can the student alter their fingertip temperature, heart rate, heart rate variability, skin conductance level, or electromyogram-measured muscle tension? It is difficult to standardize such measures, because of individual differences in baselines and differences in starting points for any given individual. Nonetheless, changes in an individual's control over these parameters over time can be documented.

The conflict resolution role-play. The student writes a conflict resolution dialogue, attempting to have each character demonstrate each of the seven criteria for conflict-resolution dialogues that are listed in the instructions on psychological skills. One point is given for each person in the dialogue who fulfills each of the 7 criteria, so the score for the dialogue can range from 0 to 14.

Fantasy rehearsal. The person is given several standard situations, and is asked to write a fantasy rehearsal of an adaptive response to the situation. The rehearsal may be rated holistically or by standard criteria. One subset of this might be to use anger control provocations, or anxiety-related triggers, as the situations in question.

Decision. The person is given a hypothetical situation and is asked to write a SOIL ADDLE story in which someone 1. thinks about the most important aspects of the **Situation**; 2. decides upon their **Objectives**; 3. gathers **Information**; 4. **Lists** options; 5. considers the **Advantages** and disadvantages of options, 6. **Decides**, 7. **Does** what what decided, and 8. **Learns** from the **Experience**.

Ethical principles. The student is asked to write for a few minutes on the question: "What rules of ethics do you think should guide people's conduct? What principles can you think of, that you would like for human beings to use to guide their behavior?" If a student can come up with nothing to say in answer to this question, education can not be succeeding very dramatically. On the other hand, students who have been taught in the way envisioned here should be able to use the 16 skills and principles, or whatever subset of them they wish, as an outline for their answer.

I believe that very important research work lies ahead in validating measures based on these tasks. If the students are asked to write their responses, then writing skill is partly measured as well as the psychological skill in question. In a group of children where writing skill is taught thoroughly enough, all students should be able to write well enough to answer these questions. Written answers solve an enormous logistic problem: rather than having to take each child out individually for testing, you can test a whole classroom simultaneously.

If it turned out that the scores on such tests were reliable and valid measures, correlating with other measures of the psychological skill in question, and if improvement on these measures generalized to improvement in the psychological skills in life, an enormous amount of good could be done.

Neuropsychological measures and exercises

The phrase "executive functioning" has become popular, possibly in part because it means so many different things. It refers to planning ahead, calculating consequences, making judgments, using self-control, set-shifting (meaning paying attention first to one variable and ignoring another, then ignoring the first and paying attention to the second, depending upon what the directions are), and various others. These functions appear to have in common their reliance upon the frontal lobes of the brain, especially the prefrontal areas, and they all appear to be diminished, on the average, in sets of people attaining the label of Attention Deficit Hyperactivity Disorder (as well as several other conditions). There are several neuropsychological performance tests of executive function, as well as rating scales; ADHD is defined by its real-life symptoms. As such, the concept of executive

190

function provides something of a link between abilities defined by rating scales and those defined by performance tests.

According to some researchers, task-switching or set-shifting is a skill particularly difficult for people with lower executive functioning skills. A typical set-shifting task is one in which, for example, the following task is used. A testee is shown a figure with a certain shape and color; two figures are shown below, one matching the figure above with respect to shape, and one with respect to color. The testee is given a direction to "match on color," ignoring shape. But after doing this, perhaps for several trials, the testee is now asked to "match on shape," ignoring color. The testee has to hold in working memory the answers not only to "How do I do this?" but also to "What am I supposed to do?" Being able to save a portion of neuronal processing for the question of "What am I supposed to do" rather than just doing it may protect against impulsivity.

Another task-switching exercise is the Stroop task. Words such as pink, green, red, and blue are displayed in some color other than the one named by the word. Sometimes the question is, "What color is the word," and sometimes the task is "Read the word." The user has to set-shift between the two directions. In a similar task, the user has either 1, 2, 3, or 4 digits displayed on the screen, and those digits are either 1, 2, 3, or 4. Sometimes the question is "How many numbers are there," and sometimes the question is "What number is displayed?" For example, if 3333 is displayed on the screen, the answer to "What number?" is 3, and the answer to "How many numbers?" is 4. Again, the user has to set-shift between two aspects of the stimulus.

Can performance on neuropsychological tests of frontal lobe functioning be improved by repetitive practice? Some research studies suggest the answer to this is yes, and it would indeed be surprising if practice could not improve such skills. But the bigger question is, would "frontal lobe exercise" of this sort generalize to real-life challenges, such as resisting impulses, making rational decisions, and sustaining attention? My guess from experience so far is that such generalization, if possible at all, would require a very large amount of "frontal lobe exercise." But more moderate quantities of such exercise, when combined with all sorts of other psychological skills exercises, may be helpful.

Performance measures of work capacity

Another aspect of self-discipline that is somewhat different from set-shifting and other aspects of executive functioning is what we might call work capacity, persistence power, or mental stamina. It may consist of two separate parts: the ability to keep working on a mental task for a long time *without* feeling a lot of boredom, restlessness, or fatigue, and the ability to keep working *despite* feeling boredom, restlessness, or fatigue. A high work capacity is obviously very useful for success, academic or otherwise.

A way of measuring work capacity is various versions of "continuous performance tests." The task is not

192

exciting. As an example, letters are flashed upon a computer screen, and the testee must press a space bar each time a letter other than X appears on the screen, but withhold this response when the letter X appears. There is no feedback about whether responses are correct or incorrect. In some versions the testee has to persist in this task for a little over 14 minutes. Informally, I have found the student's subjective reaction to a task such as this to be a useful piece of information. The students who feel that it is an absolutely horrible experience because of how bored, tired, or restless they felt, tend to have problems with schoolwork.

The problem with this task is that it is hard to give it many times, and teach to it. Why should students spend time on a useless task like this, when there is so much useful practice that can also exercise the anti-boredom capacities?

Accordingly, we can give repetitive, mentally demanding work that is actually useful to do. The student works at academic drills keyed to his or her level of ability, and the computer keeps track of the speed and accuracy of the work. The student is periodically asked for a subjective rating of how much "persistence power" is left.

The following are the tasks on these measures:

1. Vocabulary learning. The level of the program is set according to the difficulty level of the vocabulary words. The student is presented with a sentence with a blank to fill in with one of 4 words. The words are presented along with their definitions, so that if the student does not know the

meaning of the word, reading the definition to decide which word belongs in the blank helps the student learn the word.

2. Spelling. The level is set according to the length of the word. The program presents four words in a chunk for the student to master. The program first presents a word, one at a time, for the student to type, with the word remaining on the screen while it is typed. Then the program flashes the words briefly on the screen for the student to type. After cycling through the four words for a couple of repetitions each, the program moves to four more words.

3. Touch typing. The same spelling program can be used to teach students touch typing. At the beginning, there should be someone there to make sure that the student uses the correct fingers with the keys. The touch typing program starts off with typing asdfg and hjkl;. These are the home keys. The next level moves to the diagonals: aqaz, swsx, dedc, frfv, gtgb, hyhn, jujm, kik, lol., and ;p;/. After this the learner types the alphabet, then short words, then longer words and copying of text.

4. Math facts. The level may be set. The program presents math facts, and the student types or selects the answer.

5. Multiple choice questions. With this program, the user answers multiple choice questions. There may be instructional material written above or below the question, instructing the user in the knowledge necessary to answer

the question. This program can be adapted for a variety of subject matters, including reading comprehension.

The computer programs that I consider ideal for such self-discipline training are at the 1980s or 1990s level of complexity – without distractors, with simple presentations on the screen, simple requests for responses, and simple feedback to the responses.

These sorts of tasks lend themselves to research questions. First: do students' performances on such tasks correspond to teacher ratings, grades, and other measures of persistence power and sustained attention? Second: how long must the test be, to get a valid measure of persistence power? Is this different when the test is given at the beginning of a school day from when the test is given at the end of a school day? When a student has fatigued himself by such a mental task, what types of experiences tend to restore the student's persistence power most effectively: exercise, socialization, a snack, or a meditation session? The answer very likely depends upon the deprivation state of the particular person: exercise for those who have been kept sitting, rest for those who have had strenuous exertion, socialization for those who have done solitary work, solitude for those who have had much interaction, nature for those who have been looking at screens.

But the major research questions are the following: by letting students practice such tests repetitively, can we build up the persistence power "muscle?" (Self-discipline has been compared to physical strength: self-discipline is fatiguable in the short run, but exercise of this ability increases it in the long run.) If we build up persistence power with measures such as these, will that buildup in persistence power generalize to other academic tasks, such as doing homework, writing papers, and studying for tests? If the answers to these questions are favorable, a great deal of good could be done for students.

Here's a vision: at regular intervals, a student at school sits down to the computer to do a persistence power test. There is a graph of the previous performances, and the student shoots to break the record and make the graph slope upward. There is lots of social reinforcement and celebration when a new record is set, and higher performance than before is a joyous occasion. My guess is that both self-discipline and academic skills would be enhanced by this; the question of how much is one that research should answer.

Ratings of the learner's attitudes toward learning

Perhaps the most important outcomes of education are hardly ever measured: how much does the learner like to learn? How much does the learner enjoy reading, writing, math, psychological skills studies, or other activities? How much does the student enjoy school? How pleasant is it to interact with others at school? How curious does the learner feel, to find out more about the world and human beings? After "finishing" a course, how much does the student want to remember what was learned and find out more about the subject?

In therapy sessions, I have heard numerous students tell me, "I *hate* math." Yet those same students spend hours on videogames at levels of challenge which, if I attempted them without preparation, would probably be as frustrating to me as math is to them.

Why try to make subjects enjoyable to students, other than the basic ethical principle that it's more desirable to inflict pleasure than pain? Learners who are having fun will be much more likely to behave better. Learners who enjoy learning will learn better at the moment. And importantly, learners who get positive emotional associations with the activities will want to continue them even when they are no longer coerced to do so. I would estimate that at least 90% of what I know, that I find valuable, has been learned outside of formal schooling. Without the positive emotional associations, that learning would have been stunted.

The conclusion is that we should be asking students to rate their emotional responses to what is going on at school. Their ratings may be overly dependent on what happened in the last 15 minutes, or whether they are mad about something unrelated, etc. Still, such ratings are much better than nothing. Such ratings can be done by questionnaire or by interview. Which of these is more useful probably depends on how much the student can trust the interviewer.

"Teaching to a test" can be good

In some school districts there is so much pressure on teachers to obtain high test scores that "teaching to the test" replaces other activities that would make school more meaningful and a richer experience.

But part of the problem may be that we are testing too narrow a range of skills. When we are able to measure psychological skills as well as we measure academic skills, teaching to those "tests" will probably be extremely good uses of time.

Chapter 13: Useful Work

What's a typical day for students? They go to school, turn in homework, take tests, and have work returned. They come home and do homework, play video games, sometimes play with other people, sometimes do competitive sports, perhaps watch a movie or TV, and go to bed. There is no dearth of entertainment in life. Yet life often feels empty and meaningless; this idea comes through despite their difficulty articulating it.

What's missing from this sort of life? One of the main things is *useful work*. I use this phrase not to refer to work that is useful in preparing to help humanity a few years from now, but to work that directly causes benefit to someone as soon as it is done.

Useful work may be one of the most gaping holes in contemporary youth culture. Throughout most of human history, children have been relied upon, even compelled, to help with the work that the family had to do. Help with hunting and gathering, or with agriculture, began as soon as the child was physically able to do it, for prehistoric culture and most of recorded history. Children in past eras may have thought, "I am being exploited," or "I don't get to rest and play enough," but they probably did not think, "My life makes no difference to anyone," or "I see no results of any of my effort." The wild plants that they helped gather, or the beans they planted, served to help their families survive. But with the end of the brutal exploitation of children that came with child labor laws in the 20th century, and the movement from an agricultural economy where children's labor was valued, to an industrial and information-oriented economy where children had little or no place, the role of children as providers of useful work changed drastically.

In today's world, children have three main roles: as performers of schoolwork, as sports competitors, and as consumers of entertainment. Adolescents often define themselves into groups according to which brands of entertainment they prefer. They seldom see as part of their identity the provision of truly immediately useful services to anyone else.

I believe that the negative psychological consequences of the lack of useful work are probably much greater than most people appreciate. I conjecture that the need to affect other people, to make a difference to others, is a basic human motive, and if this motive is not satisfied in constructive ways, it may be manifested in destructive ways, such as bullying, annoying stimulus-seeking, aggression, and so forth.

Let's envision some of the useful work that children could learn to do during a school day. Is there snow removal that needs to be done? Snow removal can be done by a cadre of students equipped with shovels. Does the school have grass that needs to be cut, or landscaping that should be done? Pushing a non-motorized lawnmower is a great way to get exercise, and a good deal safer than playing football.

What about involving students in the effort to clean up after themselves? Sweeping and mopping floors is a mildly aerobic chore; in my own dwelling I sometimes make sweeping more aerobic by running in place while doing it. Cleaning bathrooms is a job that can be done by students with proper personal protective equipment, and need not be unpleasant in those circumstances.

Are meals cooked and served at school, and are dishes washed? What about teaching students to carry out these activities? Part of education should include the ability to actually move things and do things in such a way that a process works, not just to regurgitate information. The preparation of successful meals fits that requirement perfectly.

When repairs are made or remodeling is done to the physical plant, what about taking along one or two students as apprentices, to learn how to make the repair? What if every handy-person who carried out repairs were also trained in teaching students to do so, and in any necessary safety precautions? What if videos of repairs were made and used to teach students how to make those repairs the next time, under the supervision of an expert?

If the school has land attached that is tillable, what about cultivating a garden, right on the school property, that will result in food that can be preserved and eaten by students themselves, or given to the community?

The biggest obstacles to these endeavors are probably legal liability concerns and the need to use every minute to prepare for standardized tests or athletic contests. I hypothesize that a school that gets all students doing useful work would reap great psychological benefits. It will be a mark of great progress in society when school students can do a great deal of useful work without the fear of lawsuits standing in the way.

Not the least of the benefits would be the opportunity to put forward the idea that no useful work is "beneath" anyone – that any type of work that serves others is work to be proud of. Physical work that provides exercise accomplishes two things at once. And the attitude that I would recommend making very explicit is: we all have a drive to affect our fellow human beings; let's fulfill that drive by involving ourselves in useful work. Useful work should not be available just to the students on vocational education tracks.

In this chapter I haven't even mentioned useful work in the main enterprise of a school: education. The efforts and labor of students can be very effectively harnessed in educating other students. This portion of useful work is important enough to deserve its own chapter.

Chapter 14: Learners Who Are Teachers

There are many published studies of students' tutoring other students; almost all that I have seen report quite positive results for both learner and tutor. Yet tutoring of students by students remains one of the most underutilized resources in education.

When we are searching for useful work for students to do in school, tutoring other students is the most prominent option. Academic work is what students know how to do from their training in school. There is a large supply of both students who can use help learning academic skills, and students who can (if suitably trained) provide it.

Furthermore, the skills involved in tutoring include almost all psychological skills. The tutor must be productive enough to stay on task, joyous enough to make the task as fun as possible for the learner, kind enough that the learner feels supported, and so forth. There is hardly a psychological skill that does not come into play while carrying out the job of tutoring. Thus if we teach students to be excellent tutors, we are simultaneously teaching them to be psychologically skilled human beings.

We further benefit the tutor by the principle that "If you would learn something well, teach it." When the tutor has responsibility for imparting knowledge to a learner who is depending upon him and consciously or unconsciously judging his competence, there becomes a new motive for learning, understanding, and coming to be able to explain well.

The advantage of tutoring, from the tutee's point of view, is that the magic of one-on-one work becomes available in much greater quantity. The tutor is able to find the correct place on the hierarchy for the individual student; and if the tutor can joyously reinforce the tutee's progress and effort, the tutee gradually learns to incorporate self-reinforcement with a similar melody into his repertoire. The tutee gets many more chances to respond and practice in individual tutoring than in most classroom sessions.

Skills of the tutor

How, in general, should tutors behave? The following rating scale specifies tutor behaviors that have seemed most conducive to success in my tutoring operations so far.

Rating scale for instructors

Rate the instructor's success on each of the following, on the following scale:

0=None
2=Very little
4=Some but not much
6=Pretty much
8=High
10=Very high

_____1. Friendliness. How much was the instructor very friendly and kind to the student?

_____2. Enthusiasm. How much was the instructor enthusiastic, energetic, cheerful, and upbeat in general attitude?

_____3. Approval for the positive. How successfully did the instructor watch for the best things the student did, find some, and give very enthusiastic approval for them, within split seconds of when the student did the good things?

_____4. Avoiding unnecessary disapproval. How successfully did the instructor avoid giving unnecessary disapproval to the student?

_____5. Nonbossiness. How successfully did the instructor avoid being too bossy with the student?

_____6. Authority. How successfully did the instructor establish and continue the precedent that the instructor's directives are to be obeyed, that the instructor is to be treated with respect?

_____7. Responsiveness to conversation. How well did the instructor encourage conversation between the instructor and the student, particularly by being responsive to any conversational utterances the student made? (Responsive means follow-up questions, reflections, facilitations, positive feedback.)

_____8. Right level of difficulty. How well did the instructor choose activities at approximately the right level of difficulty for the student, and make the activities harder or easier depending on how the student did at them?

_____9. Right time on a task. How well did the instructor set a reasonable goals for time on each task for this student? How well did the instructor make the ends of tasks contingent on goal attainment and not on complaints or signs of boredom from the student?

_____10. Response to missed questions. If the student answered a question incorrectly, how well did the instructor give accurate feedback, telling the right answer instead of disapproving of the student, or continuing to request the answer from the student? Did the instructor sometimes reinforce trying, rather than getting the right answer?

_____11. Pacing of activities. How well did the instructor maintain a pace of the activities that was fast enough not to bore the student, but not so fast as to create a rushed atmosphere?

_____12. Response to undesirable behavior. How well did the instructor follow a reasonable decision tree in responding to undesirable behavior by the student? (Strategies to try: Ignore; calmly explain to the student

what he should do, and why; end the session with
expressed hopes of more cooperation next time.)

_____13. Mastery of activities. Did the instructor
demonstrate full and smooth mastery of any activities that
the instructor was leading? That is, how well did the
instructor do each of the activities?

_____14. Avoiding arguing. Did the instructor avoid
arguing with the student? Reflections, ignoring, silence,
positive feedback on the student's thoughtfulness, attempts
at rational joint decision-making – all of these and more
are alternatives to getting into an adversarial conversation.
The tutor's job is to pick good options when the student
offers provocative utterances.

_____15. Differential reinforcement. Did the instructor
show the student lots more attention, excitement, and
interest when the student was doing something desirable
than when the student was doing something neutral or
undesirable?

_____16. Valuing work and achievement. How
successfully did the instructor make comments that
communicated the philosophy that work and achievement
are good things?

_____17. Monitoring. Did the tutor do any activities that
helped, in an ongoing way, to monitor whether the student
is getting better and better at the most important skills for

the student? (Exercises provide monitoring, as well as rating of the student's behavior in the session, or getting ratings from the student or a teacher or parent. More formal tests also provide monitoring.)

Written instructions for tutor training

Many of these items are fairly subtle to define and to carry out. How does one stay in authority without using the negative tones of voice and nagging behaviors associated with the word bossy? It's possible, but not all can do it right way. How does one know in advance the right goal to set, so that the tutor does not reinforce the student for complaining of fatigue or for mental fatigue itself by stopping only when the student complains, but yet set a high enough goal that the student is challenged and stretched? These and other aspects of tutoring are not simple. Tutors should get lots of instruction, and should study textbooks before launching their intervention. My book, *Manual for Tutors and Teachers of Reading,* is an example of such a textbook, as is *Guidelines for Psychoeducational Tutors.* There are further guidelines in my book, *Psychoeducational Tutoring.* Letting tutor candidates carefully read instruction manuals and take tests over them is a first step in training tutors.

Monitored role-playing

After the tutor does the book-learning to criterion, the tutor practices the activities in role-playing. We want the tutor candidate to practice doing things the right way from the very beginning; thus it's important that the tutor candidate see proficient models and have their initial practices closely monitored. Tutor candidates continue role-played practice until the tutor has gotten much positive practice of every situation that is likely to come up at the beginning of tutoring. In carrying out monitoring, corrective feedback, and decisions as to whether the criteria have been reached, it's important that the trainer of tutors be expert in the tutoring techniques that are taught. Classroom teaching does not automatically train one to be an expert one-to-one tutor. In fact, some classroom teachers get into habits of using disapproving tones of voice a large fraction of the time; many get into habits of persevering on whatever the lesson plan for the day is, regardless of whether it is too hard or too easy for the learner. Given the luxury of one-on-one, the tutor can afford to be more joyous and more flexible in hierarchy-ology than many classroom teachers habitually are.

Specific activities for tutoring

What is to be the content of tutoring? There are various possibilities, depending upon the age and stage of the tutee.

Reading

I believe that in the best of circumstances, every middle school student who is capable of it would be taught to be an expert tutor of reading, and would be assigned to a kindergarten or first grade student to tutor individually. Teaching reading is an enormously useful and easily measurable skill. It is perhaps the most important academic skill goal in all of education. It is gratifying for both tutor and tutee. The way to do it successfully has been well researched. The process of tutoring entails both drills that build self-discipline, and stories that can model psychological skills and be entertaining.

I have written about the process of tutoring reading in *Manual for Tutors and Teachers of Reading*.

Alternate reading of psychological skills manuals

At any time after learning to read well enough, students can begin to read psychological skills manuals aloud, alternating with the tutor. The "primer stories" in *Manual For Tutors and Teachers of Reading* are meant to provide the very first experiences of text reading, while at the same time modeling psychological skills. *Illustrated Stories that Model Psychological Skills* provides a next level of reading difficulty, with each story modeling one or more skills. Of the progammed manuals I've written, *Programmed Readings for Psychological Skills* and *A Programmed Course in Friendship Building and Social Skills* are the two of easiest reading level. After that, *A Programmed Course in Conflict-Resolution and Anger Control*, *A Programmed Course in Self-Discipline*, *A Programmed Course in Anxiety Reduction and Courage Skills*, *A Programmed Course in Psychological Skills Exercises,* and *Ranks and Challenges for Psychological Skills, Student Manual,* can follow. *Learning the Math Facts with the Broken Number Line Method* and *Reading About Math* can allow tutor and student to work on math together. And *Manual for Being a Successful Student* covers study skills and organization skills for students. Comprehension probes, one per page, similar to those in the programmed books have been prepared for several trade books: a few of the *Boxcar Children* books, *Mrs. Frisby and the Rats of NIMH*, *The One and Only Ivan*, *The Peace Seekers*, *Bud, Not Buddy*, and abridged versions of the *Secret Garden*, *Hans Brinker*, and *Great Expectations*. An excellent programmed series on English grammar has been created by Joseph Blumenthal, entitled English 2200, English 2600, and English 3200.

Psychological skills exercises

The psychological skills exercises are much more fun when a tutor and tutee do them together, taking turns. For example, with the twelve thought exercise, they take turns thinking up examples of the different thoughts. For brainstorming options, they take turns thinking of options. For the reflections exercise, one speaks while the other reflects, and then they switch roles. The tutor can monitor over time the student's proficiency at the various psychological skills exercises.

Computerized drills with the tutor

In learning self-discipline skills, a very important step on the hierarchy is for the student to practice the computer-assisted drills, with a tutor sitting beside him, using differential reinforcement in response to his performance, celebrating his broken records, and, in the case of the adaptation of the spelling program for touch

211

typing, making sure that the student uses the correct fingers on the keys.

Vocabulary tutoring

Vocabulary is the bottleneck for many students in reading comprehension. To comprehend, one has to: 1) be able to call out the words, 2) know what the words mean, 3) focus and think well enough to put the words together to make meaning. A large enough vocabulary is extremely helpful for not only for reading and writing, but also for thinking: it is much easier to think about a certain idea if you have words for it in your vocabulary. Tutors and students can use any of a number of instruction books on vocabulary, taking turns with exercises.

Telephone tutoring

Many tutoring activities can be conducted as well via telephone as in person. Telephone tutoring allows the benefits of tutoring to go on without the logistics of transportation getting in the way. Telephone tutoring is a way for the sessions to take place daily. With daily sessions, review can occur before the student has had as much of a chance to forget the previous learnings. In schools where tutoring skills are taught to large numbers of students, some of them may want to have a part time job doing telephone tutoring with a student outside their school. The Organization for Psychoeducational Tutoring, Inc. (OPT) is a nonprofit that delivers this. For more about this, see optskills.org.

Supervising tutoring

Three aspects are necessary (but not sufficient) for tutoring to be successful: training, process accountability, and outcome monitoring.

As described above, training for tutors consists of reading the tutoring manuals, being tested over them, and then role-playing the tutoring activities to the criterion level.

Process accountability means monitoring the tutoring sessions to make sure that they are occurring regularly enough and for a long enough time; that the tutor is using differential reinforcement well via tones of voice; that the activities are at the correct level of difficulty for the student, and so forth.

And outcome monitoring means that there is regular measurement of the skills that the tutoring hopes to promote, to see if they are increasing.

These aspects of supervising tutoring take time, energy, and organization. But the benefit to both tutor and tutee make the effort more than worthwhile. Supervising and monitoring of tutoring, like tutoring itself, is a complex skill that nonetheless over time can be taught to students.

Chapter 15: Cooperative Games and Sports

In competitive games, one player's gain is another's loss. I want to score as many points as possible and keep your score as low as possible; your goals are the direct opposite of mine. The structure of the game is set up that one side's success makes the other side unhappy.

In cooperative games, the players have the same goals. What makes one player happy also makes another happy. The more successful any player is, the greater the chance of success in the joint effort.

Schools in our culture promote competitive sports, often with much more fervor than they promote anything else. Some colleges are much more widely known for their athletic teams than for their academics. The success of athletic teams sometimes brings about more support from alumni than does the success of the scholars.

The competitive sport fervor that prevails is, I believe, a consequence of the millennia of evolution in which human beings bonded themselves into small tribes which attacked and defended themselves from other tribes. Competitive "team spirit" had great survival value. Sports teams are, according to this theory of evolutionary psychology, proxies for small armies.

But if the human race is to move beyond a world where, in the words of Matthew Arnold, "ignorant armies clash by night," a cooperative spirit must be fostered and nurtured. The evolutionary module in the human brain for cooperation is also present and capable of being cultivated. Perhaps some of the following cooperative sports and activities would nurture this spirit.

Hiking and cross-country running

In these cooperative activities, the walkers and runners do not race each other; they keep each other company and have pleasant conversation during the sport. These are quintessential cooperative activities.

Cooperative basketball

Two people are best for a team, although three or four at a time can also play. You mark a spot about thirty feet from the basket. The first person shoots, and gets the rebound, while the second runs behind the marked spot and back toward the basket. The first person passes to the second. The second person shoots and gets the rebound while the first is running behind the marked spot and back to the basket.

The two players alternate like this for three minutes. The object of the game is for the team to make as many baskets as possible in three minutes. However, baskets only count when the person or people who did not make the basket congratulate the person who made it, and that person says, "Thank you!"

The players may want to do lots of three-minute trials, attempting to break their previous records.

Maximum hits volleyball

You play a regular game of volleyball, with any number of people on each team. But in this game the object is to see how many times you can hit the ball before it touches the ground. Alternatively, you can start a timer and see how long you can keep the ball in play. A good variation, especially for indoors, is to play with a beach ball or a balloon. With a beach ball, you can take an impact right in the face without it hurting!

A variation when there are several on each team is that each time you hit the ball over the net, you go under or around the net to play on the other side. Another variation is not to use a net and let anyone hit the ball to anyone. Maximum hits tennis or table tennis can be played in the same way.

Maximum distance soccer

There are teams of two players. You mark out a path. This can be a path through the woods or from one place to another on a field. If the players reach the end of the path before the time it up, they turn around and come back to the beginning, and then go back again. You set the timer for three minutes. The two players must alternate kicks—that is, no player can kick the ball twice in a row. The object of the game is to go as far as you can in three minutes.

Towel push-ups

One person does push-ups. The other two people help the person. The two helpers do so by putting a towel under the chest of the person who does push-ups. Each of the two helpers grasps one end of the towel. They lift up when the person is coming up and lower when the person is going down. The person has to straighten out the arms altogether at the top of the push up and move the angle at the elbow past a right angle at the bottom of the push up. The object of the game is for the team to complete as many push-ups as possible in the time allotted.

The best way to maximize the number of push-ups is for the two helpers to coordinate their efforts with each other and with the person doing the push-ups.

Rope jumping

A great cooperative activity, practiced beautifully on many inner-city playgrounds, has two people swinging two ropes in two directions, and a third person between them, jumping. This maneuver is difficult, and it's good to work up to it by steps. One person can practice jumping by himself; three people can practice rope-jumping using only one rope. For a full-length book on the fine art of rope-jumping, see *The Jump Rope Book* by Elizabeth Loredo, Workman Publishing.

Trailmaking

This is a game for the woods. Each person, or each group, marks a trail through the woods in some way that does not harm the environment: for example, making pointers with stones or dead wood, or with little bits of flour. Then the person or group that didn't make the trail gets to try to follow it. The trailmakers can come along behind the trail followers to see how successful their markers were, and offer help if needed. The trailmakers can leave some sort of treasure hidden at the end if they wish.

Navigating with topographical maps

You get a good topographical map of a region of woods and a good compass. You find some place in the woods and start there. You figure out from the map exactly which direction it is to a certain other landmark (i.e., how many degrees) and how far it is. You then use the compass to walk in exactly the direction you need to go, for about the distance you have figured, and see whether you can find the other landmark.

Here's a variation. The leader takes the group into the woods by a circuitous route. The leader shows the group members where they are on the map. The group then takes the map and compass and finds their way out of the woods.

Rhythm

You sit in a circle and clap twice on the thighs and twice with the hands. Everyone gets this rhythm going. Then someone starts by saying his name twice (during the leg claps) and then saying someone else's name twice (during the hand claps). The person whose name was called, without breaking the rhythm, calls out his name twice on the hand claps and someone else's name twice on the leg claps. You keep going without breaking the rhythm as long as you can. You vary the speed to keep the challenge in the best challenge zone for the least skilled players.

What am I doing?

You make a list of activities such as the ones below, and write them on pieces of paper. You put them in a pile. You take turns picking one from the pile and acting it out. The audience tries to guess what the person is doing.

Variation: You don't make a list, and you take turns, with each person both making up something and acting it out.

List: Brushing teeth. Playing a piano. Playing a guitar. Shooting an arrow. Digging a hole. Petting and playing with a dog. Driving a car, and calling someone on a cell phone while doing so. Feeding some fish in an aquarium. Milking a cow. Paying for something at a check-out line by swiping a credit card through a card reader and then signing the receipt. Waiting for a bus, seeing the bus coming, and getting on the bus and sitting down. Knocking on a door, being let in, and greeting your host. Putting sunscreen on your skin. Getting a big bunch of laundry and starting to put it on hangers and hang it up. Eating spaghetti. Finishing taking a big test and turning it in. Asking someone to dance, but getting turned down. Sawing a piece of wood. Hammering a nail. Drying dishes and putting them away. Playing a hand-held video game. Being a man shaving off his mustache. Pushing a shopping

cart at the grocery store and putting groceries in it.
Feeding a baby with a bottle.

What does he like?

You can use either regular playing cards, or a
special deck of sixty-four cards with
one, two, three, or four
red, yellow, green, or blue
squares, circles, plus signs, or triangles.
One person decides upon the rule for what the
imaginary person from another planet likes and doesn't
like. For example: with an ordinary card deck, he likes
hearts and diamonds but doesn't like spades and clubs. Or
he likes even numbered black cards. With the special deck,
maybe he likes cards if they are either green or brown and
made up of stars.
After the rule-maker decides what the imaginary
person likes, the rule-maker starts sorting cards into two
sets: those that the person likes and those that he doesn't
like. The guesser tries to infer the rule by noticing what the
liked cards have in common, that is, how they're different
from the disliked cards. The challenge for the rule-maker is
to pick a rule of the degree of complexity and difficulty
that is just right for the person inferring the rule. This game
presents similar challenges to those appearing on various
IQ tests.

Password

One person thinks of a word. He tries to help the other person guess the word by saying a different word to him. If the other person can't guess on the first round, the person gives a second word on the second round. They continue until they decide to give up or until the second person has guessed.

Twenty questions

One person thinks of something. The other asks yes or no questions to try to find out what it is. The name of the game comes from the custom of having a limit of twenty questions to find out what it is, but keeping track of the count is of course inessential. The strategy in this game is to start with broad categories (E.g. Is it alive?) and gradually home in on more specific things.

Round robin story

One person starts out telling a story. Then he or she stops and lets the next person tell the story for a while. Then the telling passes to the next person, until they are done. Variation: Someone transcribes the story as it goes along.

Charades

People write sayings or titles of books, movies, songs, etc., attempting to choose phrases that the other group members will be familiar with. (Variation: you can use psychological skill-related terms, such as productivity, listing options, celebrations, positive fantasy rehearsal, and so forth.) These are all put into a pile. People take turns picking one and acting out the phase, usually syllable by syllable, while the others guess. Charades has a system for letting the audience know how many words are in the phrase, which word you are acting out, how many syllables are in this word, and which syllable you are acting out. If you don't want to bother with this, the actor can say all this verbally.

Academic contests against Mr. X

Someone comes up with a set of questions or problems that are at the right degree of difficulty for the contestants. The subject area can be math, science, spelling, or any other area. (For elementary or middle school children, you may want to take a look at the *Spectrum Test Prep* series, or the "Brain Quest" questions.)

The real humans play against Mr. X. They take turns attempting to answer questions. One person is asked the question but can collaborate with any other person. For each correct answer, the real humans get a point. For each incorrect answer, Mr. X gets from two to five points, depending on how difficult the questions are. To increase the stakes, you can make it so that the humans give themselves a reward of some sort if they win, but not if Mr. X wins.

Cooperative chess

The two people collaborate in playing against a computer opponent whose skill level is set at approximately the same level, or a little lower than, that of the humans. The two people alternate in making moves against the opponent. They can talk with each other freely about which move is best. They see how high level an opponent they can jointly beat.

In a different variation, the two people take on a series of chess problems such as those in the drills in computer chess programs, or in chess books. The level of difficulty of the problems must be carefully chosen. They take turns giving the answer, but they can consult freely with each other. The two people can see how many problems of a certain type they can solve correctly in a certain time, and then attempt to beat their record.

Cooperative freecell

Freecell is a solitaire card game. A computer version was included as an accessory on past versions of Microsoft Windows. The game is also available in other computer versions. It can even be played with real cards! It is an all-time great solitaire game, because it depends upon skill and not primarily upon luck, and because most hands are winnable if people will think ahead carefully. The hands of the Microsoft computer version are numbered, so that you can pick easy hands (e.g., #8), and you can replay the same hand as many times as you like.

In the cooperative version, two people play, taking turns making moves. They can talk with each other all they want about strategy. Both win if all the cards can be moved from the original stacks to the final ones.

This alternating strategy can be used with many other solitaire games.

Mastermind

This can be played in a competitive version as a commercially available board game. It can also be played noncompetitively, in the context where players take turns solving the problem that the other one makes up. It can be played without equipment, in the following way.

One person, the code-maker makes up a four-digit number, consisting of any permutation of the digits 0 through 5. The code-breaker writes down a guess for a four-digit number. The code-maker responds by writing, beside that guess, two numbers. The first number answers the question "How many digits in the guessed number are both correct and in the correct position?" The second number answers the question "How many are the correct digit but in the incorrect position?" The code-breaker contemplates this feedback and makes another try. They continue until the correct number is guessed.

Having four digits and six possibilities for each digit is just one way to play the game. For younger code-breakers, or for code-breakers who don't feel like working their brains so hard, you can use fewer digits for the answers or fewer possibilities for each digit.

Ballroom dancing

In this activity, the proficiency and success of each partner adds to the success of the other rather than subtracting from it. This is a great chance for males and females to practice cooperation with one another. Folk and square dancing provide similarly cooperative activities. A variation is for students not to partner up, but to learn steps and for everyone to do them together.

Singing in harmony

Singing songs with two or more harmonious parts is easier than most people think it is; it is a prototypical cooperative activity. Instructional recordings can help in the learning process.

The shaping game

The Shaping Game is one of the best cooperative games. In this game, one person (the shaper) writes down a behavior that he or she wants the other person (the shapee) to do. The goal of each person is for the shapee to perform the behavior. The only way that the shaper can give clues is to positively reinforce the shapee for things the shapee has already done. Thus the shaper says things like, "I like it that you looked that way!" "I'm glad you turned that direction." "That's nice that you touched the desk." "I'm glad you picked up the book on the desk." "Hooray, you opened the book! You read from it! That's it!" One of the goals of playing this game is to help the participants learn "internal shaping," where they deliver self-reinforcement through their internal speech, as they make successive steps toward a goal.

Useful work

Any and all of the activities mentioned in the chapter on useful work can be cooperative activities.

More thoughts on cooperation

There is definitely a place in the world for competitive attitudes as well as cooperative attitudes. There are times when opposing the will of another person is the most rational and reasonable choice.

However, we live in a world where competitive attitudes between nations, and the resulting bellicose actions, threaten to exterminate the human race. Many people live in families where constant competitive bickering and rivalry between siblings produces an emotional climate dominated by hostility. Many marital relationships are characterized by the same state in which the partners stay opposed to each other. Relationships among school children are very frequently marred by too much hostility and competitive attitudes.

If you want to have people feel good about one another, which sort of game makes more sense: one where one person beats the other, or one in which they work together to accomplish a mutual goal?

In 1961 a group of researchers led by M. O. Sherif reported the "Robber's Cove Experiment." A highly competitive set of games between groups of children at a summer camp created growing rivalry and hostility between the children, even outside the context of the games. When the hostility had reached a high level, the experimenters were able to reverse the ill effects they had produced. They did this by halting the major competitions and scheduling activities that promoted cooperation between former rivals. Ethics committees will probably prohibit any repetition of this experiment.

My prediction is that parents, teachers, camp directors, employers, and others in charge of groups will be able to promote more cooperation and less hostility in real life by providing higher exposure to cooperative games and activities.

Thoughts for excellence in cooperative games

Here are some thoughts to keep in mind while doing cooperative games.

1. I want to help find the correct level of challenge for all the players—not too hard and not too easy.
2. I want to celebrate my own successes.
3. I want to celebrate my fellow players' successes.
4. I want to use fortitude when I fail at any attempt.
5. I want to be supportive when any of my fellow players fails.
6. I can push myself to the limits of my ability, if I want to, even without a competitor.
7. I want to approach this game or activity joyfully.

Chapter 16: Relaxation, Biofeedback, Meditation

Our bodies are capable of a very wide range of arousal states, from the highest excitement of rage or ecstasy or giddy hilarity, to the low arousal that appears just before falling asleep, or when calmly meditating. At any given moment, some point on the spectrum of arousal is optimal for whatever goal we have at the time. But therapists constantly see people who can't relax when they want to sleep, get too nervous when they want to have calm rational decision-making, or who feel too sluggish when they would rather become highly motivated to action. A fair fraction of what we mean by arousal or excitement has to do with the activity of the sympathetic nervous system, the part that is heightened by adrenaline and noradrenaline. If only we could control our degree of arousal or excitement. But we can! It's just that very few people have ever sought to learn this, and almost no schools teach it. But this is a skill that is of utmost importance in the conduct of life.

Let's think a minute about how the skill of regulating one's degree of arousal could help solve various problems. For people with anxiety or anger control problems or insomnia, expertise in being able to turn down the level of arousal is obviously extremely useful. For people who don't get enough exercise, turning up the level of arousal so that one feels like exercising can help greatly in achieving relaxation later on. For workers, being able to turn up the level of arousal can increase productivity. In any performance situation, the Yerkes-Dodson curve refers to an inverted u-shaped graph of performance versus level of arousal; there is some level that is optimal for nearly every performance. By being able to adjust the level of arousal to the right place, it's more often possible to achieve peak performance.

The biofeedback paradigm

Biofeedback is a way to make the learning of relaxation and self-regulation skills more effective and fun. You hook up some gadget that measures a physiological parameter that you wish to control: heart rate, muscle tension, fingertip temperature, skin conductance level, and heart rate variability are the most commonly used ones. Then the student plays with making the levels go up and down, discovering the techniques that most effectively allow control of these parameters. As time goes by, the goal is that the student becomes more and more expert at making the levels go up or down at will.

A pulse oximeter gives a good readout of heart rate; lowering one's heart rate usually corresponds to greater relaxation. A thermometer with a probe that can be held between the fingertips is another inexpensive biofeedback device; higher fingertip temperature corresponds to greater relaxation. Fingertip temperature is a better index of relaxation versus arousal when room temperature is in the region of 70 to 74 degrees Fahrenheit.

Relaxation and meditation techniques

When teaching relaxation and meditation, I like to let the learner try out several techniques, and find out which is best for that particular learner. Here are some techniques:

Muscle relaxation. The student focuses attention on the various muscle groups of the body, and tries to make each of them as loose and soft and relaxed as possible. EMG (electromyogram) biofeedback can make this more fun. An important preliminary to muscle relaxation skills is figuring out how to tense, at will, the various muscle groups of the body.

The good will meditation, a.k.a. loving kindness meditation. The student thinks: May I become the best I can become. May I give and receive kindness. May I live with compassion and peace. Then the person wishes the same things for some other person. Throughout the meditation, the person wishes makes these three wishes for more and more different individuals, and perhaps for groups of people.

Imagery of kindness. The student pictures people being kind to each other by being good listeners and conversationalists, helping, complimenting, doing fun things together, being honest, and so forth.

Use of a mantra. The student uses the word *one* or some other repeated stimulus to say to himself during the meditation. If the attention strays from the mantra, that's OK; the directive is that when the learner becomes aware that he is not saying the mantra, that he should "gently swing back to it."

Awareness of the contents of consciousness. In this form of meditation, the student lets the mind start out as if a blank screen, upon which thoughts and images may appear. When thoughts and images do appear, the mediator simply accepts their occurrence, and continues to save part of the mind to observe what the rest of it is doing. This is one of several different procedures that have been called "mindfulness meditation."

Simple rest. The meditator simply sits with eyes closed and rests, without trying to do anything in particular. This technique in one study proved as useful as the more elaborate ones.

Five in and five out. Meditators look at the seconds counter of a watch or stopwatch. They start breathing in with seconds that end in 0, and start breathing out with seconds that end in 5. Thus they breathe 5 seconds in and 5 seconds out, for 6 cycles per minute. This is a very important anti-hyperventilation exercise, and hyperventilation is central to many panic attacks. In addition, the 6 cycles per minute respiration seems to activate the "rest and digest" system of the body, that is, the parasympathetic nervous system.

The pleasant dreams exercise. The meditator spins out a dream-like narrative of images of kindness, relaxation, and beauty. This is a process of composing an ongoing story, only a story without conflict and danger and excitement, but of pleasant tranquility. This is a great exercise for the meditator to do while lying in bed drifting toward sleep.

The psychological skills mediation. The meditator goes mentally through each of the 16 skills and principles, and thinks of a positive example of each of them, recycling through again when the end of the list is reached.

Meditation with movement. The "mantra" in this type of meditation is a movement that the meditator repeats. For example, you clasp your hands together in front of you and push them together or pull them apart. You move your hands down almost to the floor while bending your knees, and stretch them overhead while straightening the legs out.

In schools that teach psychological skills, each of these techniques would be taught to students, and they would be asked to experiment with each of them enough to learn which of them help them the most.

The crucial role of exercise

Except for the meditation with movement described above, meditation and relaxation techniques usually involve stillness and sitting. But in most schools, people are asked to sit way too much. The muscles of most people are not suited for relaxation until they have had a chance to tire themselves. Thus before training meditation and relaxation, schools should ideally make sure that students get large quantities of physical exercise.

Chapter 17: Music

Music and songs are linked to emotion. Sometimes people with damage to certain areas of the brain that control spoken language can nevertheless recall and sing songs. Songs are more connected with the emotions than speech. Monotone speech, devoid of melodic content, tends to be unemotional.

Music also is an aid to memory. I can remember some songs that I heard only a few times in early childhood, with no exposures since that time. Apparently lots of other people find that catchy tunes stay tenaciously in the memory bank; this is probably why advertisers often put their messages into jingles. If memory for jingles is tenacious, it stands to reason that we should make available for children some of the important principles of living, in the form of songs and jingles.

Modeling songs, like modeling stories and plays, are meant to give positive models of psychological skills, no negative models, and no resolution of anything by violence.

I've composed and recorded some modeling songs in a collection on CD called "Spirit of Nonviolence." As a biased reviewer, I think of these songs as a good way of getting positive patterns into the memory bank.

In my vision of the ideal school, groups – classes, groups of classes, lunchroom groups, the whole school – would often sing "modeling songs" together. In my vision, such group singing would not require a music expert, or a music class, or accompaniment. All it takes is someone to set the pitch and for others to join in. If the others can learn to harmonize, that is a beautiful and wonderful skill. If they sing in unison, that's great also.

Some other modeling songs

If you are on the lookout, you can find many songs that model desirable, psychologically skillful ways of thinking about the world. Once you find those songs, see if you can make them belong to your school. Below are listed some "oldies" that have appealed to me, along with the psychological skill that I perceive the song to be modeling. (Many of these were old, even when I was young!) One of the tasks a school can take on is to update this list. Students can search for songs that add to the bank of positive models, just as they search for other works.

Climb Every Mountain, by Oscar Hammerstein II, Richard Rodgers
(Sustaining Attention to Tasks, Sense of Direction and Purpose)

Edelweiss, by Oscar Hammerstein II, Richard Rodgers
(Pleasure from Blessings)

Everything's Coming up Roses, by Stephen Sondheim, Jule Styne
(Pleasure from accomplishment)

Getting to Know You, by Oscar Hammerstein II, Richard Rodgers
(Social Initiations)

The Happy Wanderer, by Antonia Ridge, Freidrich W. Moller
(Pleasure from Blessings, Social Initiations)

If I Had a Hammer, by Lee Hays and Pete Seeger
(Kindness, Sense of Direction and Purpose)

If We Only Have Love, by Jacques Brel, English Lyrics by Mort Shuman and Eric Blau
(Kindness)

Last Night I Had the Strangest Dream, by Ed McCurdy
(Conflict Resolution, Nonviolence)

May You Always, by Larry Markes, Dick Charles
(Kindness)

Mockingbird Hill, by Vaughn Horton
(Pleasure from Blessings)

My Favorite Things, by Oscar Hammerstein II, Richard Rodgers
(Pleasure from Blessings)

Oh, What a Beautiful Morning, by Oscar Hammerstein II, Richard Rodgers

(Pleasure from Blessings)

On a Clear Day, by Alan Jay Lerner, Burton Lane
(Pleasure from Blessings)

On the Sunny Side of the Street, by Dorothy Fields, Jimmy McHugh
(Pleasure from Blessings)

They Can't Take That Away From Me, by Ira Gershwin, George Gershwin
(Separation Tolerance)

This Land Is Your Land, by Woody Guthrie
(Pleasure from Blessings)

We Shall Overcome, Traditional, Modified by Zilphia Horton, Frank Hamilton, Guy Carawan, Pete Seeger
(Purposefulness, Justice in Choosing Options)

When the Red, Red Robin Comes Bob, Bob, Bobbin Along, by Harry Woods
(Pleasure from Blessings)

Who Will Buy?, by Lionel Bart
(Pleasure from Blessings)

Whistle While You Work, by Larry Morey, Frank Churchill
(Sustaining Attention to Tasks)

The World Is Waiting for the Sunrise, by Eugene Lockhart, Ernest Seitz
(Pleasure from Affection, Loyalty, Intimacy)

I Gave My Love a Cherry, Traditional
(Trusting, Intimacy, Pleasure from Affection)

I May Never Pass This Way Again, by Murray Wizzell, Irving Melsher
(Kindness)

My Way, by Gilles Thibault; Claude Francois, Jacques Revaux, Paul Anka
(Independent Thinking)

People Got To Be Free, by Felix Cavliere, Edward Brigati, Jr.
(Kindness, Toleration)

Sunrise, Sunset, by Sheldon Harnick, Jerry Bock
(Loyalty, sustained attachment)

Tomorrow, by Martin Charnin, Charles Strouse
(Positive Aim)

What a Wonderful World, by George David Weiss, Bob Thiele
(Pleasure from Blessings, Kindness)

Somewhere, by Stephen Sondheim, Leonard Bernstein

(Kindness, Forgiving, Positive Aim)

Heaven Help Us All, by Ronald Miller (Kindness)

Up On the Roof, by Gerry Goffin, Carole King (Relaxation)

Lavender Blue, Traditional (Kindness, Loyalty)

Oh Had I a Golden Thread, by Pete Seeger (Kindness, Purposefulness, Courage)

Garden Song, by Dave Mallet (Delay of Gratification, Productivity)

O Freedom, Traditional (Assertion)

Lean on Me, by Bill Withers (Depending, Kindness)

You've Got a Friend, by Carole King (Nurturing, Loyalty)

All I Really Need, by Raffi (Joyousness, Kindness, Loyalty)

Blowing in the Wind, by Bob Dylan (Conflict Resolution, Purposefulness)

What the World Needs Now, by Hal David, Burt Bacharach (Kindness)

Danny Boy, by Fred E. Weatherly, Traditional Melody (Loyalty, Separation Tolerance)

All Through the Night, by Harold Boulton, Traditional melody (Nurturing)

Day Is Done, by Peter Yarrow (Nurturing)

Morningtown Ride, by Malvina Reynolds (Nurturing)

Now the Day is Over, by Sabine Baring-Gould, Joseph Barnaby (Nurturing)

Sweet and Low, by Alfred Tennyson, Joseph Barnaby (Nurturing)

He Ain't Heavy, He's My Brother, by Bob Russell, Bobby Scott (Kindness)

Morning Has Broken, by Eleanor Farjean, traditional melody (Pleasure from Blessings)

Wild Mountain Thyme, Traditional (Pleasure from Blessings, Friendship-Building)

Song of Peace, by Lloyd Stone, Jean Sibelius (Tolerance, Conflict Resolution)

Study War No More (Down by the Riverside) Traditional (Conflict Resolution)

Baby Beluga, by Raffi (Nurturing)

If I Only Had a Brain, by E.Y. Harburg, Harold Arlen (Humor)

Shake My Sillies Out, by Raffi (Gleefulness)

There But For Fortune, by Phil Ochs (Empathy)

You Can Get It If You Really Want, by Jimmy Cliff (Sustaining Attention, Delaying Gratification)

Let's Get Together, by Chet Powers (Kindness)

I Love the Mountains, Traditional (Pleasure from blessings)

When You and I Were Young, Maggie, by George W. Johnson, J.A. Butterfield
(Loyalty, sustaining attachment)

Peace Train, by Cat Stevens (Nonviolence)

Flow Gently, Sweet Afton, by Robert Burns (Kindness)

I Would Be True, Traditional (Honesty, courage, fortitude, kindness)

Chapter 18: Art

I mentioned earlier some very repeatable assignments for students, that were along the lines of "write something worth writing," "read something worth reading," and "do some math that you think is at the right level for you." In this chapter we add another: "do some art that you feel is worth doing, and if you choose, tell about it." By "do some art," I'm here referring to drawing, painting, sculpting, collage-making, craft-making, doing computer assisted animation or illustration, and the like. (I save dance, drama, poetry, fiction, and music for other discussions.) Furnishing a variety of art materials and providing some instruction in techniques, e.g. how to represent three dimensional reality on a two dimensional surface, can enhance the enterprise.

What makes such activity worth doing? There seems to be an inherent worth in self-expression, for representing what is in the mind. People's wishes to put their mind's workings into the form of visual art have been apparent since prehistoric times. For children, having the opportunity to explain in words anything that they wish to explain about artistic creations can enhance the experience greatly, and can open up channels of communication. Without the experience becoming "art therapy," it's probably nonetheless helpful if children can have some degree of privacy when talking about their artistic creations.

In addition to this useful open-ended procedure, Two art activities fall into the category of extremely useful work.

The first is the creation of illustrated modeling stories. If the school takes seriously the project of growing the Bank of Positive Models, there should be many positive modeling stories available. Students choose a story from the Bank of Positive Models, break it up into pages with not much text on each page, and illustrate each page. The drawings could be scanned into computer files (if not done on the computer in the first place) and used in the construction of illustrated books. These books, in turn, could be used for younger students.

The second art activity is the creation of movies that model and explain psychological skills. One way of doing this is by using student actors. Another is by creating videos of spoken stories, with illustrations. Using computer animation programs is another option. Another technique involves using toy people or puppets to create recorded dramas. Again, this would be "useful work," designed to be watched joyously by younger (or same age) students, who would receive positive models while watching.

One problem with these activities is that students are likely to be influenced greatly by the popular culture, constructing their works of art to be attention-grabbing or slapstick rather than dignified (though possibly humorous) examples of positive psychological skills. A prerequisite for such activities is a good deal of thought and instruction about how the goal is not to make something like what appears in comic books or on television – the goal is to do something much better than that.

Chapter 19: Punishment Versus the Four Rs

How do we respond to bad behavior by students? Nearly every school adopts some method of punishment: detentions, suspensions, time outs, and so forth.

An alternative to traditional punishment is what I have called the Four Rs. The student is asked to respond to the situation in as constructive a way as possible.

Before presenting the Four Rs, let's imagine that you, an adult, fail to pay attention to your driving well enough (while fiddling with an audio player in your car) and rear-end another car at a traffic light. This is certainly undesirable behavior.

What sort of corrective action would you take upon yourself for this careless behavior? How about making yourself sit in a place and do nothing for a while? Giving yourself an electric shock? Getting someone to yell at you? Putting yourself in the stocks? Jailing yourself (at taxpayers' expense) for a few days?

Most of us would probably not find such punishments very constructive to inflict upon ourselves. Let's instead imagine what the Four R's would be in response to this behavior:

1. Responsibility. The first step is saying, "This was my responsibility. I realize that you did not back into me; I bumped into you."

2. Restitution. I make restitution to the other driver by getting their car fixed (or getting my insurance company to finance such).

3. Redecision. I decide: what do I want to do in the future, to avoid events like this? I need to keep my eyes on the road, and only pay attention to the an audio player when I am stopped.

4. Rehearsal. I do lots of fantasy rehearsals as follows: I'm driving in my car, and I get the urge to fiddle with the audio player. But then I think, no, that can wait. I need to keep my eyes on the road. I do so. Later, I stop at a traffic light that just turned red. Hooray, now I have time to fiddle with the device safely.

The advantage of the four R's is that the behavior done in response to the mistake or failure can mitigate the harm on this occasion, and reduce the probability of harm in the future.

When students in school misbehave, one option is to guide them through the steps of the Four R's. A mistake or failure provides lots of opportunity to construct many fantasy rehearsals of the skill that is opposite to the mistake or failure. It is even more useful to teach students about these steps in a lesson not associated with a mistake or failure, to prepare them, during calm moments, for the time when they will use the steps.

Chapter 20: Culture and Emotional Climate

A school environment, like most other groups of people, gradually takes on a personality of its own. The behaviors of each individual influence the interpersonal climate of the group, and likewise each individual is influenced by the group climate. For example, one prominent element of a group climate is the tones of voice that people predominantly use with one another. Each individual models for the rest of the group, and the group models for the individual.

What elements do we desire in the emotional climate? Here are some:

1. Prevailing tones of voice of enthusiasm and approval and celebration of accomplishments both of oneself and others.
2. Much productivity, goal-driven activity – not just hanging out.
3. An alternation between self-discipline requiring activities and activities that replenish the stores of self-discipline.
4. Open reference to the values and skills and principles that are revered by the organization; speaking about these when celebrating.
5. A climate where students help each other, and feel good about helping each other.

6. A climate where people like it when other people make accomplishments. This is a cooperative climate rather than a totally competitive climate.

7. A climate of fun, enjoyment, and pleasure in life and in the activities of school.

How do people achieve a certain emotional climate or interpersonal culture for their school? Here are some possibilities:

1. Public displays of positive models, both of people outside the school, and people within the group.

2. Public readings about the skills and principles the group reveres.

3. Public speeches by students on examples of psychological skills.

4. All school assemblies of various sorts.

5. Group singing of songs that celebrate psychological skills.

6. Affirmations regarding psychological skills, and public unison reading of these.

7. Public pledges. Rather than, or in addition to, pledges of allegiance to a flag, students and staff can repeat pledges to strive to greater psychological skill.

8. Periods of silent meditation on the skills and principles in large groups.

9. Award ceremonies, recognizing people for their achievement in psychological skills growth.

10. Faculty as participants, as growers, learners of psychological skills, who learn along with the students, rather than posing as perfect in the skills, but:

11. The selection of faculty members who embody the skills and principles as thoroughly as possible, from the beginning.

12. Attempts to get parents in as much as possible on the process of learning psychological skills and celebrating their growth in their children.

13. Conscious attention to the interpersonal climate of the group, and asking how it can be improved. For example, asking students to discuss this topic or to write about it.

Poor climates abound

I saw an advertisement for a research project recruiting teachers. The project examined the teachers' vocal cords, looking at the prevalence of laryngeal polyps, presumably caused by teachers' raising their voices at students so often. I have heard teachers screaming at students at such high volumes that the teachers would have been at very high risk for laryngeal polyps.

Even when teachers do not yell at students, what is the prevailing tone of voice that they use? What is the prevailing facial expression? Do they look happy? Are they smiling? Does their tone of voice convey approval or disapproval? For many schools where I've been, the tones of voice and facial expressions generated by staff members are primarily disapproving. The ratio of disapproval to approval is quite high.

Why does such a situation exist? I understand, from personal experience, the reinforcement contingencies that lead teachers to voice lots of loud disapproval. The teacher walks into the classroom, and students are loudly talking with one another, enjoying their socializing. The teacher says, in a quiet voice, "May I have your attention?" The students ignore the teacher, and can't even hear him, because of the noise they are generating. The teacher now affects an angry face and says loudly, "I said, give me your attention, and that means stop talking now!" The students decide that he means business and stop talking. The teacher has now received a very powerful reinforcer – the attention of his students. And the behavior that has been powerfully reinforced is angry, loud, commanding.

Over time, the students may habituate to a disapproving utterance of loud commanding, and the teacher may need to escalate the show of disapproval. Often the students and teacher go down this road of reinforcement and habituation until the teacher is screaming just to get the students to pay attention.

Part of the problem in this scenario is that the teacher is trying to get students to do things they really don't want to do. They would much rather socialize with each other than sit silently and listen to what the teacher has to say. They are much more powerfully reinforced by the interest and attention of their peers than by the approval of the teacher when they do stop talking and pay attention. They come to see the teacher as someone who gets them to stop doing fun things and start doing boring things. They begin to see themselves in an adversarial relationship with the teacher. How much can they get away with? How much socializing can they do when the teacher's back is turned?

If there is a prevailing emotion of anger between students and teachers, this must have a strong negative influence on the emotional climate among students themselves. They imitate to some extent the tones of voice that they hear the most, and if adults are angry, they tend to be angry with each other.

In addition, there are other influences predisposing to a negative emotional climate. Many sensation-seeking students find themselves bored by academic work, and find the default method of getting stimulation to be taunting or teasing another student and provoking a strong negative emotion in response. Even the students who are not sensation-seekers may find themselves more entertained by watching such an interaction than by doing whatever else they were doing.

There is probably an innate tendency of human beings, most obviously males, to arrange themselves in dominance hierarchies, pecking orders, whereby they decide who is superior to whom. The most obvious hierarchies depend on a rank ordering of proficiency at fighting. School culture sublimates this tendency only slightly when it encourages students to strive for the highest position on the hierarchy that they can attain in football or wrestling or other combat-related sports.

Monitoring the emotional climate

The notion of an emotional climate should be an important concept, taught to all students. They should know what the marks of a positive climate are: people being kind to one another, helping each other, giving lots more approval than disapproval, cooperating on projects and ventures, having fun with each other, not needing or wanting to deceive, wishing the best for both self and others and acting on those wishes. They are familiar with the concept of each individual's contribution (positive or negative) to the emotional climate. Such familiarity should make it easier to measure the emotional climate of a classroom or the whole school, by asking the students. They can give ratings (simplest is: how good is the emotional climate, where 0 is very bad, 10 is very good, and 5 is neutral?) They can write about how good the emotional climate is, how to improve it, and what choices people have made already that have made it better or worse. They can tell about circumstances when it is good and right to sacrifice some of the agreeableness of a group, for example when the group is comforting itself with ideas or practices that are wrong. We would not have evolved the ability to contradict and criticize others if these behaviors weren't occasionally useful. Administrative and teaching staff can from time to time do interviews with students to get their ideas about the emotional climate in face to face interaction.

Chapter 21: Training for Conflict-Resolution, Anger Control, Nonviolence, and Peace

Is it reasonable to ask education to drastically reduce people's inhumanity to one another, to diminish cruelty, violence, verbal abuse, and hatred? Can education help people to do joint decision-making or conflict resolution in rational ways, and to value and to gain skill in the production of positive emotional climates? Can people be taught to achieve the ends that violence and hostility sometimes accomplish – usually interpersonal power – but to do so in nonviolent ways?

If we think of the attainment of these ends as taking place by means of skills that can be taught and learned, it is hard to imagine that these goals can be attained by any means *other* than education – although not necessarily all taking place in schools.

The following are some methods and activities whereby school activities could conceivably produce progress toward a world without violence, a world of rational joint decision-making, a world of positive emotional climates, a friendly world.

The study of nonviolence movements and nonviolence heroes

As children study history, they learn lots about great generals who were victorious in warfare – in fact, sometimes history feels like the story of one war after another. And as they take in popular literature, they become very familiar with the action and adventure heroes of the day. But how many know the stories of nonviolence heroes? How many, for example, know the story of Carl von Ossietzky, the German journalist who took a courageous stand against the rise of Hitler, and who was awarded the Nobel Peace Prize while in prison? How many are very familiar with the ideas and practices of Mohandas Gandhi, who led India to independence in through a non-war, a nonviolent struggle? How many are familiar with how formidable the task was for Gandhi, and for Martin Luther King, who was greatly influenced by Gandhi's example, to persuade followers to maintain the strategy of nonviolence? How many are aware of who the Nobel Peace Prize winners of the last few years have been, and what they have done?

In the field of peace and nonviolence, enough has been written to give reading practice throughout every year of education. At least some of such facts and ideas can and should be included every year.

Study of admiration of the violent hero

Please imagine the following plot line for a story. A very bad powerful guy, or bunch of bad guys, decide to inflict sadistic cruelty. Little do they know that they have underestimated the fighting skills of the good guy. After a suspenseful buildup, the fight begins, and after amazingly agile moves, with or without weapons, the good guy renders the bad guy(s) either dead, unconscious, begging for mercy, or fleeing.

Have I just invented an original plot line for a story? On the contrary, I have recounted perhaps the most hackneyed plot of human history: a plot that has been repeated countless thousands of times in movies, TV shows, works of fiction, videogames, scriptures, contests of combat sports, and others.. It seems that human beings never tire of the many variations of this plot. A prominent variation is one where the violent hero is not particularly good, or is obviously bad (e.g. Grand Theft Auto). The moral of the story is: become very, very proficient at violence. Get to the level where you can assert your power over predatory humans, by your superb violence skills. You'll not only be safe; people will admire and revere you.

A nonviolence curriculum in schools will do well to study what it is up against. Let's become aware of some of the many iterations of the violent hero plot that pervade our culture. Let's study how realistic the usual movie fight scene is, where the hero absorbs blows, any one of which in real life would likely result in permanent damage or death. Let's think about what, in evolution, made this story so attractive to people. Let's look at the scientific literature on what the effects are of viewing it.

And: let's be aware of the amount of self-discipline necessary to do activities such as the ones in this chapter, such as writing out dialogues of rational conflict-resolution. Let's acknowledge that it might be much more fun to watch or enact the hero overcome the predators, and be able to feel good about our choices to do the relatively less exciting activities I'm about to describe.

The bank of provocations

We build skills by practicing. A very important form of practice is with the sorts of situations that provoke anger and hostility – we can call the entire set of these, provocations. Special cases of provocations are situations where one person wants something, and someone else wants something that is seemingly incompatible: conflicts. Often conflicts are signaled when one person commands another to do something the other doesn't want to do. Criticisms are another important class of provocation – often these disapprove not just of a certain behavior, but of the entire person. Contradictions are another set: you say something, and someone tells you you're wrong, you're mistaken. There are all sorts of other provocations: impingements on our territory, unwanted noise, smells, or sights that are imposed upon us, rejections, induction of jealousy, breaking of promises, deceptions and lies, frustrations from having our progress toward a goal interrupted, and so forth.

My book, *A Programmed Course in Conflict-Resolution and Anger Control*, contains appendices with several hundred conflicts, criticisms, and other provocations listed, to practice with. Part of the mission of a school can be to expand this bank of practice situations. Students can notice the provocations in their own lives, in history and current events, in fiction of all sorts, and in their fertile imaginations, and write these down. We are aiming toward an education wherein for any provocation that a student is likely to encounter in life, the student has already had practice in thinking rationally about the response to a provocation that resembles it.

Dr. L.W. Aap dialogues

In a previous chapter I listed steps in rational conflict-resolution and joint decision-making, which can be remembered with the mnemonic, Dr. L.W. Aap:

1. **Defining** the problem in terms of one's own needs or interests or wishes, without accusing the other or commanding the other. Each person should do this.

2. **Reflecting,** or paraphrasing in an empathic way, the other person's point of view to make sure one understands. Thus the first defines and the second reflects, after which the second defines and the first reflects. In the simplest version, they do this in one sentence apiece, but sometimes much more dialogue is necessary.

3. **Listing** options for what to do – possible plans for trying to meet the needs of both people.

4. **Waiting** until they are through brainstorming options before discussing which options are best.

5. **Advantages** and disadvantages: talking about the possible positive and negative consequences of the various options, their pros and cons.

6. **Agreeing** on something, even if it's only one aspect of what the desired plan would look like, or even if it's only a plan to continue thinking and talking later.

7. **Politeness** throughout the conversation: not interrupting, raising the voice, insulting the other.

These sorts of conversations can be practiced through role-plays and through written exercises. The vision is that each student would both act out and write many, many Dr. L.W. Aap conversations in the course of education. Exemplary written products would be anthologized into books of models used to teach others how to construct these conversations.

An important variation is when one person resorts to some commands, criticisms, contradictions, threats, or other obstructive communications, as people are accustomed to doing, but the other person sticks to the Dr. L.W. Aap guidelines as much as possible to steer the conversation toward productive conflict-resolution. Written examples of this process form another important volume.

Ida Craft options with provocations

With any sort of provocation, a fundamental reflex to instill in students is generating more than one option for how to respond, and evaluating the options. Ida Craft is a mnemonic to help generate options for how to respond.

Ignoring: Not responding at all to the provocation.

Differential reinforcement: Not responding to the provocation, and trying to reinforce the behavior that it opposite to it.

Assertion: Stating one's wishes in a clear and confident but nonaggressive way.

Conflict-resolution protocol: Dr. L.W. Aap conversation.

Criticism protocol: Any of the criticism responses listed elsewhere, with mnemonic T Paarisec.

Relaxation: Using relaxation techniques to turn down the flight or fight response.

Rule of law: Appealing to authority, rules, or laws in determining what to do.

Away from the situation: Having the two people go away from one another, at least until things have cooled off.

Apologizing: Being able to acknowledge one's own mistake sometimes is the best response.

Force of nonviolent nature: Sometime physically restraining a violent person, without hurting the person, is the best response.

Friendliness: Sometimes friendly talk can defuse hostility.

Tones of voice: Sometimes speaking in soft, slow, low tones can defuse anger.

With any provocation, a written exercise can be to go through these options and others, listing options, writing about their pros and cons, and making a pitch for which option might be best. The listing and choosing process may have the effect of activating the brain regions that make rational choices, as opposed to those responsible for flight or fight. Of course, reasonable and creative options that do not fall into any of the Ida Craft categories are more than welcome!

T Paarisec with criticisms

With the bank of criticisms, students can generate various options for responses, and ponder which type of response might be best in the given situation. Some criticism responses are as follows.

Thank you: Sometimes criticism is constructive, and it's good to acknowledge the help that the criticism provides.
Planning to ponder or problem-solve: "I'll do some thinking about that."
Agreeing with part of criticism: "It's true that I'm not perfect in that way."
Asking for more specific criticism: "Tell me more about what you think I should do, please."
Reflection: "So if I understand you right, you think that I _____; correct?"
I want or I feel statement: "That may be true, but I still want _____." Or "I feel ___ about what you said, because _____."
Silent eye contact.
Explaining the reason: "Here's why I did what I did," (or want what I want, or said what I said…"
Criticizing the critic: For example, "I think you have a problem that leads you to want to insult and dominate people, that you need to work on."

The twelve-thought and four-thought exercise

As explained in a previous chapter, the twelve thought categorization is an aid to selecting what to say to oneself about a situation – the central act of cognitive therapy or cognitive restructuring. The twelve thoughts are

1. Awfulizing: recognizing the badness or danger of the situation; this can be overdone or not.

2. Getting down on oneself: recognizing the harmfulness or mistakennness of one's own behavior; this can be overdone or not.

3. Blaming someone else: recognizing the harmfulness or mistakenness of someone else's behavior; this too can be overdone or not.

4. Not awfulizing: Acknowledging that the situation can be handled, that it is "not the end of the world."

5. Not getting down on oneself: Deciding not to punish oneself more than is reasonable.

6. Not blaming someone else: Deciding not to keep recriminating the other person in one's mind.

7. Goal-setting: Deciding upon the outcome that is desired for the current situation.

8. Listing options and choosing: Generating options for responding to the situation, thinking about pros and cons, and deciding.

9. Learning from the experience: Thinking about any beneficial learnings for future reference.

10. Celebrating luck: Noticing and remarking to yourself about any aspects of the situation that are lucky for you.

11. Celebrating someone else's choice: Noticing and celebrating anything someone else has done that was positive.

12. Celebrating your own choice: Noticing and celebrating anything in your own response to the situation that was positive.

The twelve thought exercise is speaking or writing each of those twelve thoughts about a given situation; provocations can do nicely for practice, as can any other situation. The point of this is to gain practice in coming up with each of the 12 types of thoughts, so as to better select the ones that will be most useful to us. The opposite of this ability is being stuck in habits of responding in fixed ways.

The four thought exercise is a subset of the twelve thought exercise: not awfulizing, goal-setting, listing options and choosing, and celebrating your own choice. This is meant to be useful in real-life situations where there isn't time to go through all twelve thoughts. The four thoughts are a good default reflex to turn to in the face of provocations. It's useful to practice it many, many times with different hypothetical provocations.

Nonviolent sources of power

A major reason for violence, anger, or hostile expression is to exert power and influence over another person or set of people. Part of the nonviolence curriculum of schools can be the study of sources of interpersonal power that are nonviolent. For examples: the ability to

260

marshal facts and ideas articulately in a persuasive argument; having ethical principles on one's side; the ability to walk away from a deal; the ability to create bids from competitors; high work capacity; having money, resulting from savings and work habits; having valuable skills; the ability to get allies onto your side. As with all psychological skills, the topic of nonviolent sources of power and influence can be the topic of numerous written works by students.

Analysis of conflicts or other provocations

At any given time, there are numerous conflicts going on that are being written and spoken about in the news. There are numerous conflictual interactions depicted in plays, screenplays, and novels. And there are lawsuits going on, in which disputes are being aired in court. What are the needs, wishes, or interests of the parties to the conflict? What are the obstacles to peaceful conflict resolution? What communication techniques appear to be used, or is there a lack of communication? What could be options for solutions to the conflict? Which options do you think are most just?

These too can be the topics of much writing by students, and the best writings can be anthologized to help future students.

Celebrations of joint decision-making

Of course, whenever people come together, they will have conflicts of interest, and thus one can find plenty of choice points for joint decision-making among the interactions of students themselves. If they can be on the lookout for opportunities to practice rational joint decisions, and write about their own enactments of Dr. L.W. Aap, and feel good about them, that adds real-life practice to the hypothetical situation practice that forms the core of the conflict-resolution curriculum.

Eyes on the prize: Imagining a friendly world

One of the major predecessors to progress is simply imagining what life would be like when the innovation is made. Science fiction has envisioned outcomes which later came to pass – air transportation, a trip to the moon, individual communication devices, robots, artificial intelligence, and so forth. The ideal school should challenge students to imagine: what would society look like if violence, cruelty, exploitation, theft, extortion, and verbal abuse came close to vanishing? What would be the economic consequences? How could the trillions of dollars spent on defense budgets be diverted to efforts that increased the quality of life? How much could be saved by a downsizing of the criminal justice and incarceration industries? What would be the psychological consequences? How much would mental health be improved simply by the elimination of child abuse? How much improvement in mental health would come simply by elimination of bullying? What fraction of post-traumatic stress disorders would vanish if interpersonal cruelty diminished to almost nothing? If people were not scared of one another, what fun things would they be able to do that they can't at present? What if the word "stranger" were not associated with "danger," but with "a friend you haven't met yet?" How much happier would children be if not so many parents were in very bitter conflict with one another? How much more exploration and socializing could children do if parents were not so fearful on their behalf? How much more volunteering at schools could take place if schools did not need to regard every volunteer as a potential predator?

The answers to these questions provide some of the motivation for doing all the other activities of this chapter, and indeed, all the activities of this book; it is hard to imagine any one psychological skill, which if greatly improved in society, would not have positive consequences for reducing violence and increasing friendliness.

Chapter 22: Study of Mental-Health-Friendly Environments

If the environment of school can be made maximally mental-health-friendly, that is a monumental accomplishment. But one element that it very likely to increase its mental health impact is to include, within the curriculum, the study of human environments in general. What constitutes mental-health-friendly environments? How do we create and shape them for ourselves and other people? When we find ourselves in unfavorable environments, what are our options?

Let's list some aspects of the environment that have an impact on mental health.

1. Physical characteristics. Is there physical danger from other people? Are there toxins, such as lead paint chips, in the environment? Are there exposures to animals with worms or other parasites? Is there a great deal of noise? Are there loud or otherwise powerful distractions that preclude focused thought? Do such distractions interfere with sleep? Is the temperature in a favorable zone? Is there nutritious food to eat, and not much temptation from junk food? Is the air not polluted, either by toxins in the general environment, or by second hand smoke? Is good health care available and affordable?

2. Kindness versus hostility in the interpersonal system. Is the emotional climate generally positive, in the family, the neighborhood, the larger community? Is it possible to walk

around without fear of violence? Is there an absence of warfare? Is bullying very infrequent? How frequent is crime in the environment? How likely are people to help one another, to speak approvingly toward one another, to smile at one another? Is the cyber-environment (e.g. that of social media) a friendly one, where compassionate and thoughtful human interaction is practiced?

3. Economic circumstances. Is there enough income to get the things that are needed? Does economic inequality results in very wasteful expenditures by the rich and insufficient necessities for the poor? Are there jobs available that can provide a living wage and a source of meaning and purpose?

4. The electronic environment. Is it possible to escape input from an electronic medium – for example is a television playing continuously, is music playing continuously? Are video games or social media continuously tempting? Are the norms in the social group that people are continuously interacting with their phones or other screens?

5. Social support systems. Are there friends or family members who can provide companionship, support, and positive relationships? What is the status of connection versus isolation in the environment?

6. Effort-payoff systems. To what extent does the person have something to work toward, that provides a payoff?

7. Hierarchy-ology. Is what the person is working toward, or supposed to be working toward, neither too hard nor too easy, but in a mental-health-friendly challenge zone?

8. Norms regarding drug use. To what extent does the culture encourage, discourage, pressure, model, reward the use of "recreational" drugs, i.e. drugs designed to produce immediate pleasure, such as alcohol, nicotine, cannabis, cocaine, opiates, methamphetamine, psychedelics, and others?

9. Balance of work with the rest of life. Does the culture provide opportunities and models of a balance between work and leisure activities?

10. Availability of pleasant and healthy recreational activities. Does the environment provide participation in sports, music, drama, art, social gatherings characterized by sobriety, outdoor activities, games, fitness activities?

11. Norms regarding helping others. Are examples prevalent where people help other people for reasons other than economic gain?

12. Quality of models. What is the overall availability of positive models of psychological functioning? How abundant are the negative models? How easy is it to access examples of positive psychological skills?

13. What the community values, admires and reinforces. Do people in the community admire goodness, or power? Do they reinforce the people who attract attention, or those who have positive effects on the society? Do they admire proficiency in violence, or proficiency in helping? Do they admire learning, or do they celebrate ignorance?

14. Attention to ethical principles and value systems. Does the environment tend to remind people of important ethical principles and values? Is going over ethical principles in a spirit of reverence socially acceptable, or is such a practice ridiculed?

15. Exposure to nature. Do people have the opportunity, and do they take advantage of it, to be in natural environments?

16. The life of the mind. Does the environment value learning, thinking, great ideas, careful decision-making, research, reading, writing, science, math, using words well? Is there simultaneously a value placed on intellectual activity, and a lack of intellectual snobbism and shaming of those who are not inclined toward intellectual pursuits? Are written words and other works that educate and stimulate the mind readily available, and not crowded out by those aiming only at entertainment and amusement?

17. Freedom. Does the culture, and the authority structure, including the government, allow people to make and enact their own choices except when there is a very good reason

not to? Can people choose what to say, whom to associate with, how to worship or not worship, what to report as journalism, with reprisal coming only when their choices are clearly harmful or dishonestly misleading to the community at large (and not because they are offensive to whoever is in power)?

18. Sustainability and conservation. Do the cultural norms take into account future generations? Is there not widespread waste? Is the net effect of human activity on the environment positive, or toxic? Is the welfare of wildlife species taken into account?

19. Checks and balances. Is power distributed among people, and not concentrated in the hands of one person, or a small group of people? Do individuals in the system feel that they have some say in how the system operates?

20. Information versus propaganda. Do people have ready access to relatively unbiased sources of information, which are fact-checked? Do information sources avoid presenting only that which supports the perspective of one individual, or one tribe?

** ** **

What are the benefits hoped for in the study of the ingredients of mental-health-friendly environments?

First, it directs the attention of both teachers and students to the question of how mental-health-friendly their school is, and what should be changed to make it more so.

Second, it creates an agenda to teach students to be good citizens, where good citizenship may be largely defined as improving the quality of the environments, communities, and subcommunities of which one is a part.

Third, it helps students to become aware of possible negative influences of environments in their own lives, and to take efforts not to be harmed by them. One way they can do this is by developing independent thinking skills, skills of refusal to conform. These skills, for example, are of immense help in resisting a culture that revolves around drugs, including alcohol. These skills can help students to resist joining fully in the viewing and fantasy enactment of violent acts in video games. A second way that students can cope with negative environmental influences is to minimize exposure to them and to seek out subcultures where the influences are more positive. For example, a student might choose to hang out with peers who provide more positive models, less violence and hostility, more goal-oriented behavior.

Another way that students might respond is to undertake social activist approaches to improving environmental conditions. For example, students have taken initiatives to reduce bullying, to help other students who need help, to organize healthy forms of recreation, to promote life of the mind discussions, to present objective analyses of social issues, and others.

Students who have undergone very unpleasant experiences at the hands of their peer environments, community environments, or family environments, can study two divergent ways that people respond to such trauma. Some people tend to victimize others in the same way they were victimized; this has been called "identification with the aggressor." Others harness the emotional energy of their experiences toward activism, toward working toward an end of victimization. The question of how one can use the second response rather than the first is extremely important.

Some students who are still subjected to negative environments may need to make long term plans for how to escape those environments altogether: what do they need to learn, what skills do they need to get, what sort of people do they need to find, before they can escape to a different sort of world?

The final consequence of studying the ingredients of mental-health-friendly environments is that it puts the job of mental health promotion where it belongs: as something to which every member of a family, a school, a friend group, a workplace, a local community, a country, a planet, can contribute. The job cannot be left up to clinical professionals. I predict that if society ever does dramatically improve the mental health of populations, it will do so by improving the quality of environments, more than by improvement of clinical services.

As the places where children spend a large fraction of their waking hours, throughout their development, schools are crucial environments to make mental-health-friendly. That has been the purpose of this book. It is my fond hope that readers of this book will find some success in this crucial task for humanity.

Appendix 1: The Psychological Skills Axis

Group 1: Productivity
1. Purposefulness. Having a sense of purpose that drives activity
2. Persistence. Sustaining attention, concentrating, focusing, staying on task
3. Competence-development. Working toward competence in job, academics, recreation, life skills
4. Organization. Organizing goals, priorities, time, money, and physical objects; planfulness

Group 2. Joyousness
5. Enjoying aloneness. Having a good time by oneself, tolerating not getting someone's attention
6. Pleasure from approval. Enjoying approval, compliments, and positive attention from others
7. Pleasure from accomplishments. Self-reinforcement for successes.
8. Pleasure from your own kindness. Feeling pleasure from doing kind, loving acts for others
9. Pleasure from discovery. Enjoying exploration and satisfaction of curiosity
10. Pleasure from others' kindness. Feeling gratitude for what others have done

11. Pleasure from blessings. Celebrating and feeling the blessings of luck or fate

12. Pleasure from affection. Enjoying physical affection without various fears interfering

13. Favorable attractions. Having feelings of attraction aroused in ways consonant with happiness.

14. Gleefulness. Playing, becoming childlike, experiencing glee, being spontaneous

15. Humor. Enjoying funny things, finding and producing comedy in life

Group 3: Kindness

16. Kindness. Nurturing someone, being kind and helpful

17. Empathy. Recognizing other people's feelings, seeing things from the other's point of view

18. Conscience. Feeling appropriate guilt, avoiding harming others

Group 4: Honesty

19. Honesty. Being honest and dependable, especially when it's difficult to be so

20. Awareness of your own abilities. Being honest and brave in assessing your strengths and weaknesses

Group 5: Fortitude

21. Frustration-tolerance. Handling frustration, tolerating adverse circumstances, fortitude

22. Handling separation. Tolerating separation from close others, or loss of a relationship

23. Handling rejection. Tolerating it when people don't like or accept you, or don't want to be with you
24. Handling criticism. Dealing with disapproval, criticism and lack of respect from others
25. Handling mistakes and failures. Regretting mistakes without being overly self-punitive
26. Magnanimity, non-jealousy. Handling it when someone else gets what you want
27. Painful emotion-tolerance. Avoiding "feeling bad about feeling bad."
28. Fantasy-tolerance. Tolerating mental images of unwanted behavior, confident that you will not enact them

Group 6: Good decisions

6a: Individual decision-making

29. Positive aim. Aiming toward making things better. Seeking reward and not punishment
30. Thinking before acting. Thinking, rather than responding impulsively or by reflex, when it's useful to do so
31. Fluency. Using words to conceptualize the world: verbal skills
32. Awareness of your emotions. Recognizing, and being able to verbalize your own feelings
33. Awareness of control. Accurately assessing the degree of control you have over specific events

34. Decision-making. Defining a problem, gathering information, generating options, predicting and evaluating consequences, making a choice

6b: Joint decision-making, including conflict resolution

35. Toleration. Non-bossiness. Tolerating a wide range of other people's behavior
36. Rational approach to joint decisions. Deciding rationally on stance and strategies for joint decisions
37. Option-generating. Generating creative options for solutions to problems
38. Option-evaluating. Justice skills: Recognizing just solutions to interpersonal problems
39. Assertion. Dominance, sticking up for yourself, taking charge, enjoying winning
40. Submission: Conciliation, giving in, conceding, admitting one was wrong, being led
41. Differential reinforcement. Reinforcing positive behavior and avoiding reinforcing the negative

Group 7: Nonviolence
42. Forgiveness and anger control. Forgiving, handling an insult or injury by another
43. Nonviolence. Being committed to the principle of nonviolence and working to foster it

Group 8: Respectful talk, not being rude
44. Respectful talk, not being rude. Being sensitive to words, vocal tones, and facial expressions that are

accusing, punishing, or demeaning, and avoiding them unless there is a very good reason

Group 9: Friendship-Building
45. Discernment and Trusting. Accurately appraising others. Not distorting with prejudice, overgeneralization, wish-fulfilling fantasies. Deciding what someone can be trusted for, and trusting when appropriate
46. Self-disclosure. Disclosing and revealing oneself to another when it's safe
47. Gratitude. Expressing gratitude, admiration, and other positive feelings toward others
48. Social interaction. Starting social interaction; engaging well in social interaction or play; listening well; using tones of enthusiasm and approval; knowing what is "appropriate," and not, to say and do.
49. Reasonable expectations. Not having unreasonably high expectations from relationships; not feeling too entitled. At the same time, being able to insist on being treated justly; not tolerating abusive or unreasonable behavior from the other.
50. Sending value messages. Being able to communicate to the other that they, and the relationship, are valued, through channels that the other can receive.

Group 10: Self discipline
51. Self discipline. Delay of gratification, self-control. Denying yourself present pleasure for the sake of achieving a worthy goal

Group 11: Loyalty
52. Loyalty. Tolerating and enjoying sustained closeness, attachment, and commitment to another; keeping promises and commitments. Repairing rifts in relationships. But also deciding when it is not ethical to give advantages to friends or family members, and deciding whom you don't owe loyalty to.

Group 12: Conservation
53. Conservation and Thrift. Preserving resources for ourselves and future generations. Forgoing consumption on luxuries, but using resources wisely. Financial delay of gratification skills

Group 13: Self-care
54. Carefulness. Feeling appropriate fear and avoiding unwise risks to oneself or others
55. Habits of self-care. Healthy habits regarding drinking, smoking, drug use, exercise, diet, sleep, medical and dental care, exposure to noise, avoiding sunburn, and others.
56. Relaxation. Calming yourself, letting the mind drift pleasantly and the body be at ease
57. Self-nurture. Delivering assuring or care-taking thoughts to yourself, feeling comforted thereby

Group 14: Compliance
58. Compliance. Obeying, submitting to legitimate and reasonable authority; but also deciding rationally and ethically when not to obey

Group 15: Positive fantasy rehearsal
59. Imagination and positive fantasy rehearsal. Using fantasy as a tool in rehearsing or evaluating a plan, or adjusting to an event or situation. Avoiding having fun with violent imaginings.

Group 16: Courage
60. Courage. Estimating danger, overcoming fear of non-dangerous situations, handling danger rationally
61. Depending. Accepting help, being dependent without shame, asking for help appropriately
62. Independent thinking. Making decisions independently, carrying out actions independently

Appendix 2: Psychological Skills Inventory: Functional Assessment Version

The purpose of these questions is to let you rate how well someone has been functioning in life, over the past month. You can rate each area here, using any number from 0 to 10.

1. Productivity

For this area, think about work on a job for someone outside the family, on chores for the family, and academic work for school. Think about how much work the person can accomplish, how efficiently, and how much supervision (or reminding, or prodding, or reinforcement) is required from someone else.

0=Capable of no work at all.

2=Capable of fairly little work, and requiring constant supervision by someone else for the work to get done; work is inefficient.

4=Capable of moderate amounts of work, with constant supervision, or small amounts of work with less than constant supervision

6=Capable of fairly large amounts of work, with constant supervision, or moderate amounts of work with less than constant supervision

8=Capable of very large amounts of work with constant supervision, fairly large amounts of work with less than constant supervision, or reasonably large amounts of work with no supervision. Is efficient.

10=Very large work capacity – able to accomplish very large amounts, very efficiently, and able to do it independently, with no attention from a supervising person.

Productivity rating=_____

2. Joyousness

For this area, think about how cheerful and happy versus depressed and sad the person acts and feels, and what fraction of the time the person acts and feels that way.

0=Severely depressed and sad, all the time.

2=Depressed and sad almost all the time.

4=More unhappy than happy.

5=Neutral, pretty even balance of happiness and unhappiness.

6=More happy than unhappy.

8=In good spirits, happy, cheerful a large amount of the time, definitely enjoying life.

10=In good spirits, cheerful, and happy almost all the time. Is still capable of feeling bad when bad things happen, but not out of proportion to how bad it is, and bounces back quickly.

Joyousness rating=_____

3. Kindness

In rating this item, think about the balance between kind, helpful acts and mean, selfish acts.

0=No evidence of caring about the welfare of others, totally selfish, even enjoys making others feel bad
2=Selfish, mean, uncaring with few exceptions
4= More unkind than kind, but helpful and supportive acts from time to time
6= More kind than unkind, fairly frequent helpful and supportive acts.
8= Many more kind acts than hurtful acts, very helpful and supportive to others
10=Almost always very kind and helpful to others, almost never selfish. Very oriented to making people happy. (Can still be capable of appropriately sticking up for his or her own way and receive this rating.)

Kindness rating=_____

4. Honesty

In rating this item, think about how easy it is for the person to lie, cheat, or steal, that is how little guilt the person would have about these acts, and also how often the person does dishonest acts.

0=Not to be trusted at all. Lies, cheats, steals with the only restraint being whether he or she can get away with it, and does such acts very often.

2=Can lie, cheat, or steal with little or no remorse, and does these acts fairly often.

4= Can lie, cheat, or steal without much remorse, and does such acts often enough to be a problem

6= Has a conscience which resists lying, cheating, or stealing, and does these acts fairly seldom, but is still not "very trustworthy"

8= Has a well-developed conscience, and is trustworthy, although like most people may be capable of dishonesty when given a strong temptation

10=Extremely well-developed conscience, is extremely trustworthy. Would be completely honest except in those unusual circumstances where truth-telling would be unethical.

Honesty rating=_____

5. Fortitude

Fortitude is the ability to handle not getting what one wants, to take frustrating situations, not to be devastated by bad events, not to let negative emotion such as anger or distress or sadness hamper dealing with the world. In rating this item, think about how little it takes to distress the person, how disabled the person is by distress, and how frequently the person is disabled by negative emotion.

0=Very small events cause very disabling distress, very often, with the result of great unnecessary suffering or impairment of functioning.

2=Small events cause disabling distress often, with the result of a good amount of unnecessary suffering or impairment of functioning

4=Fairly often has negative reactions out of proportion to the event

6=Sometimes has negative reactions out of proportion to the event, but can also handle unwanted events OK fairly often

8=Ability to handle unwanted events is good, a strength

10=Ability to handle unwanted events is exceptional. Thinks about how to solve the problem, takes appropriate action, does not let negative emotion get in the way. (The person can still feel appropriate negative emotion and get this rating.)

Fortitude rating=_____

6a. Good decision-making

0=Very bad judgment. Very frequently makes very bad decisions with harmful consequences.

2=Bad judgment, bad decision-making frequently.

4=Decision-making skill could use lots of improvement. Sometimes makes decisions well, sometimes not.

6=Decision-making skill is pretty good, but makes his or her share of mistakes.

8=Decision-making skill is a strength. Generally thinks before acting and comes up with very reasonable choices.

10=Is exceptionally good at decision-making. Never, or almost never, does impulsive actions which are later regretted. Comes up with good and creative solutions to problems.

Good decision rating=_____

6b. Good "joint decisions" or conflict-resolution

Joint decisions occur when people decide together what they are going to do. They each have their own wishes, and they also have to take the other person's wishes into account. Sometimes these are disagreements or conflicts, and sometimes they are just times when people need to decide what both will do together. The highest development of this skill involves being able to state one's own point of view, listen to the other's point of view, think of creative options for solving the problem, recognize the fair and just options, and talk about advantages and disadvantages politely and with good reasoning. The good conflict-resolver has a balance between the ability to stick up for one's own way and to give in.

0=No ability to resolve conflicts rationally with other people. Either totally avoids dealing with them, or is so aggressive that communication does more harm than good.

   2=Usually quite ineffective in dealing with conflicts or making joint decisions.

   4=Skills of communication and problem-solving are not highly developed, but sometimes simple giving in or holding firm get the problem solved well enough sometimes

   6=Skills of communication and problem-solving could use much improvement, but giving in or holding firm get the problem solved much of the time.

   8=Has a good development of the skills of communication and problem-solving, and this helps the person get along with others.

   10=Is exceptionally good at all the parts of the joint-decision process. Is a good listener, creative problem-solver, polite but assertive negotiator, able to make very good decisions about holding firm and giving in. (Conflict-resolution can still be unsuccessful, when the other person does not cooperate.)

Joint decision or conflict-resolution rating=_____

7. Nonviolence

   This item has to do with any form of hurting someone else's body: hitting, kicking, scratching, biting, using weapons. This item also includes humane treatment of animals. In rating this, take into account the frequency of violent acts and the severity of these acts.

0=Very severe problems with violent behavior.
2=Bad problems with violence.
4=Pretty big problems with violence.
6= Some not very harmful violent behavior, (e.g. hitting) but not very much.
8=Violent behavior is not a problem.
10=Violent behavior is not a problem, and the person is a strong believer in nonviolence as a principle, so that violent behavior is not likely to ever be a problem.

Nonviolence rating =_____

8. Respectful talk

Nonviolence had to do with physical hurting of other people. This item has to do with verbal hostility and aggression to others, such as threats, name-calling, insults, ridicule, humiliation, bossiness, and others, versus tactfulness, politeness, respect, understanding, and kindness in one's talk. Think about the severity and frequency of hostile talk, versus the degree and frequency of friendly talk.

0=Verbal hostility is a very severe problem, frequent and intense.
2=Verbal hostility interferes greatly with relationships.
4=Fairly frequent hostile words

6=Some hostility but more often respectful talk than not

8=Does a good job of respectful talk, with infrequent exceptions

10=Is polite, respectful, tactful, friendly as a consistent habit. (This doesn't mean that he or she never expresses anger, in an appropriate way.)

Respectful talk rating = _____

9. Friendship-building and social skills

This item has to do with how well the person can have good social conversation, make friends, form relationships, get to know people in a positive way.

0=Not able to make friends at all; social skills are totally inadequate

2=Ability to make friends is limited by social skills problems

4=Able to meet people and get along sometimes, but not very well

6=Able to meet people and get along fairly well

8=Able to make friends, talk with people, and get along well

10= Is very skilled at social conversation, is outgoing, and makes friends extremely easily

Friendship-building and social skills rating = _____

10. Self-discipline

This item has to do with the ability to resist pleasurable temptations in order to meet a goal, to work for long-term goals rather than being sidetracked by short-term pleasures. It has to do with choosing to work instead of play, save instead of spend, eat healthy food instead of better tasting junk, stop doing pleasurable things when it's necessary to do so, avoid drugs, avoid overuse of videogames or TV, plan ahead, use healthy habits, and so forth.

0=No signs of self-discipline; does whatever is most pleasant at the moment

2=Only a little evidence of self-discipline

4=Some times where he or she passes up short-term gain for longer term gain, but not many

6=A fair number of times where the person passes up short-term gain for a longer term payoff, although lots of the other kind of example too

8=Evidence of good skill in self-discipline

10=Extremely self-disciplined: able to set goals and meet them, resisting almost all temptations that would get in the way of those goals

Self-discipline rating =_____

11. Loyalty

Loyalty is the ability to keep commitments to people. Some of those commitments are formal promises, and others are the expectations that reasonably come from friendship. The person who sticks up for friends and family members despite lots of social pressure to go against them has good loyalty skills.

0=No loyalty. Relationships are dropped easily. The person "uses" people and does not honor commitments at all.

2=Little loyalty. If he or she makes friends, is rejecting of those friends when other people go against that friend, or when the friend doesn't do what's desired.

4=Some loyalty but not very large amounts.

6=Feels the commitment of friendships, and fairly often sticks by those commitments.

8=Is generally loyal. Will resist some social pressure to stick by a friend or relative; will honor commitments even when it takes some personal sacrifice.

10=Is extremely loyal. Will resist the strongest social pressure to stick by a friend or relative; will honor commitments even when it takes great sacrifice. (The person can get this rating even when the person can get out of bad relationships, or fail to honor unreasonable expectations of others. There are times when one should not favor friends or family members, in the interest of fairness.)

Loyalty rating =_____

12. Conservation

This is the skill of not wasting time money, things, or the earth's resources. It includes saving money rather than spending it immediately. It also refers to the ability to have concern for the environment, to try to take care of nature, to try to live in ways that make life sustainable.

0=No interest whatever in either saving, caring for the environment, or preventing waste.
2=Very little interest in saving, caring for the environment, or preventing waste
4=Some, but not much interest conservation goals
6=A moderate amount of concern about conservation goals
8=A good amount of concern about conservation goals
10=Great concern and very positive personal actions in conservation goals

Conservation rating =_____

13. Self-care

This item has to do with health and safety habits: diet, exercise, avoiding pleasure-giving drugs, getting adequate sleep, taking care of teeth, wearing seat belts, avoiding risky activities, being safety-conscious.

0=Is a very strong risk-seeker, and gets much positive pleasure from dangerous activities, in a way that poses severe danger

2=Is a risk seeker and gets pleasure from danger

4=Can be careful at times and doesn't strongly seek out danger, but is not very concerned about health or safety

6=Follows some health and safety rules, is appropriately cautious much of the time, but could be lots better at self-care

8=Has good habits of self-care, with few exceptions

10=Has exceptional skills of self-care. Does what's best for health and safety, consistently. (You do not have to be so cautious as to interfere with the enjoyment of life to get this rating.)

Self-care rating = _____

14. Compliance

Compliance is the ability to follow rules and laws and commands of a reasonable authority, or rules that have been agreed upon. It is the same as obedience. Parents and teachers and community laws are the sources of most of the need to obey. Compliance skill includes not blindly obeying authority when it gives a command to do something that isn't right.

0=Seems to enjoys defiance. Defies authority often in very major ways. This is a severe problem for this person.

2=Noncompliance is a big problem. Compliance skills quite low.

4=Some compliance but often fails to comply.

6=Complies a fairly high fraction of the time, but there is lots of room for improvement

8=Good compliance skills. Occasional putting off or ignoring of a direction, but compliance is not a problem.

10=Exceptionally good compliance skills. Very conscientious about following reasonable rules and obeying reasonable commands. Does not have to be asked twice to do things. (One can still have the skill of ignoring or refusing commands that are wrong or unethical.)

Compliance rating =_____

15. Positive fantasy rehearsal

If a person spends lots of time in fantasies or pretend play of very antisocial behavior (especially violence), that subtracts from the functioning rating, even if the person has never so far acted out these fantasies. In rating, think about how unacceptable the imagined actions are, and how frequently they are imagined. "Fantasies" include watching television and movies and playing video games. This item refers to violence as entertainment, not to studying about violence in order to help end it or in the study of history etc.

0=Engaging in very violent or otherwise antisocial fantasies in a very large fraction of his or her free time.

2=Violent or otherwise antisocial fantasies a large fraction of free time.

4= Violent or otherwise antisocial fantasies a significant part of free time

6= Violent or otherwise antisocial fantasies some of the time, but not much

8=Avoids violent or otherwise antisocial fantasies a large fraction of the time, close to all the time. Is also able to use positive fantasy rehearsal to practice important skills.

10=Avoids violent or otherwise antisocial fantasies whenever possible, for principled reasons having to do with reduction of violence in the world, and for reasons of compassion for the victims of violent behavior. Is also very able to use positive fantasy rehearsal as a technique in gaining important skill.

Positive fantasy rehearsal rating =_____

16. Courage

Courage skills mean not having the enjoyment of life or performance of tasks impaired by anxiety and fears. Avoiding something because of unrealistic fear is the type of impairment that this item asks about.

0=Anxiety makes this person constantly avoid things, to the extent that the person is greatly impaired in functioning or enjoyment.

2=Anxieties impair functioning or enjoyment to a fairly large extent

4=Anxieties impair functioning in one specific area to a great extent, or in several areas to a moderate extent

6= Some anxiety that makes life less pleasant or successful, but not much of the time or not very severe

8=Anxiety is not usually a problem. Perhaps occasional infrequent anxiety of a mild sort.

10=Anxiety is not a problem at all. The person is quite confident. (Having this rating does not mean that the person does not avoid actual danger or have realistic fears.)

Courage rating =_____

Appendix 3: Psychological Skills Inventory, Short Form

Please rate how well the person is functioning in each of these areas.

0=Very undesirable, very great need for improvement.
2=Definitely undesirable, great need for improvement.
4= In the undesirable range, need for improvement.
6=OK, adequate, acceptable, but not great. Improvement is desirable.
8=Good functioning in this area. Would be just fine if pattern continued as is.
10=Excellent functioning in this area. Would be great, wonderful if pattern continued as is.
n=Not applicable, not answerable, or not known

_____1. Productivity. Being able to invest sustained effort toward a worthwhile end.

_____2. Joyousness. Being able to enjoy working toward goals, being with other people as well as being alone, and being able to sustain a sense of morale. Having a sense of humor.

_____3. Kindness. Wanting to make other people happy, taking pleasure from helping others be better off, having a sense of conscience that resists making others unhappy.

_____4. Honesty. Truthfulness, avoidance of deceit.

_____5. Fortitude. Handling adversity and frustration in a rational way.

_____6. Good decisions. A: Individual decisions: Going through a systematic mental process to decide the best thing to do.

_____6B: Joint decisions or conflict-resolution: deciding rationally upon a joint course of action with another person or group of people.

_____7. Nonviolence. Avoiding killing and hurting except as an absolute last resort.

_____8. Respectful talk. Except when there is a very good reason not to, communicating with others in the least hurtful ways possible.

_____9. Friendship-building. Meeting people, making friends, enjoying the art of social conversation, building relationships over time.

_____10. Self-discipline. For the sake of accomplishing goals, being willing to forego pleasure or endure discomfort.

_____11. Loyalty. Honoring commitments; having a reasonable sense of obligation to people who have earned it; at the same time knowing when it is not ethical to give advantage to one's friends and family.

_____12. Conservation. Being thrifty, not wasteful, in the use of time, money, and things; working toward the nonwasteful and sustainable use of the earth's resources.

_____13. Self-care. Having good habits of health and safety, including diet, exercise, drug or alcohol use, accident-prevention; looking after one's own welfare. Also being careful about the welfare of others.

_____14. Compliance. Doing one's part toward promotion of the rule of law. Following and obeying rules, and complying with legitimate authority, except when it is unethical to do so.

_____15. Positive fantasy rehearsal. Avoiding entertaining oneself with fantasies or fictions of cruel and violent and maladaptive actions, unless there is redeeming benefit. Using fantasies of positive patterns as a way of practicing them.

_____16. Courage. Reducing any unrealistic fears and aversions one finds oneself held back by. Not letting fears get in the way of doing what is best.

.

Appendix 4: Sample Psychological Skills Book Report

Here's a sample book report on *Les Miserables* by Victor Hugo.

Four acts of self-sacrificing kindness are pivotal events in the plot of *Les Miserables*.

The first is carried out by Monsieur Myriel, the Bishop of Digne. Formerly a man of wealth, the bishop has taken up a life of service and renunciation of material possessions. He has retained only a set of silverware and some silver candlesticks from his formerly wealthy life. When the former convict Jean Valjean is rejected by all others when he seeks lodging, the bishop gladly provides it; he also treats the former prisoner with great courtesy.

Hardened, however, by his years of punishment, Jean Valjean steals the bishop's silverware in the night and leaves the house. When he is caught and returned to the bishop's house, the bishop performs a transforming act of kindness. He saves Jean Valjean from life imprisonment by stating that the silverware is a gift; he gives the former convict the candlesticks as well, with a "reminder" of a promise (that Jean Valjean didn't really make) to use the gift to become an honest man.

Does the bishop make a good decision? How many times would such an act actually transform a criminal, rather than "enable" him to do further stealing? We must keep in mind that, though hardened, Jean Valjean was not a selfish criminal. He was sent to prison originally because of the theft of bread to feed someone else, not himself. Perhaps the bishop had enough discernment skills to realize the capacity for goodness and sacrifice that Jean Valjean had, underneath the bitterness induced by years in the galleys.

Jean Valjean escapes the reputation of an ex-convict by living under an assumed name. He becomes a highly successful businessman and the mayor of a town, due to his intelligent decisions and productivity. But then a difficult choice point arises: an innocent man is identified as Jean Valjean and stands to be punished severely for a minor crime.

Jean Valjean must wrestle with a moral dilemma of kindness versus self-care. In the second pivotal sacrificial act of kindness, Jean Valjean displays his courage as he dramatically reveals his true identity in the courtroom, freeing the innocent man, but becoming, from that point on, a fugitive from "justice."

Could he have used options other than betraying the innocent man or sacrificing his own place in society? With his ample money, he could have used excellent lawyers or bribery to try to win the man's freedom. He could have arranged a daring escape for the innocent man and set him up with a pleasant life far from the jurisdiction. But the author doesn't allow Jean Valjean (who is strong and good, but not usually a clever schemer) to escape to options that would allow him to "have his cake and eat it too"; he must choose between the innocent man and himself.

As a fugitive, Jean Valjean rescues Cosette, a girl who becomes his foster daughter; for many years, he lives a life of dedication to her. Meanwhile he is pursued by inspector Javert, whose moral development has reached only the level of rigidly following the rules. Javert is incapable of seeing the goodness of Jean Valjean, but focuses only on the fact that he is wanted by the authorities.

In the midst of a failed rebellion, Javert is captured by revolutionaries who owe a favor to Jean Valjean. Jean Valjean asks to be able to execute Javert. But instead of killing him, he fakes the execution and frees Javert. He thus performs the third pivotal act of kindness, benefiting the man who is the biggest threat to his own happiness. There is no ulterior motive in this act. Jean Valjean is simply not a murderer, and does not tolerate murder, even of his worst enemy.

Javert later is faced with a moral dilemma of compliance versus loyalty: by law, he is supposed to capture Jean Valjean, but Jean Valjean has saved his life. Javert escapes this dilemma by suicide. This is obviously a negative example of the skill of decision-making. Decision-making is most difficult in this sort of situation, where all options conflict with strongly held beliefs or feelings. But Javert would clearly have been better off allowing Jean Valjean to go free, and working on gradually reducing any guilty misgivings about a kind act for this good man.

The failed rebellion injures a young man named Marius, who has fallen in love with Cosette. Marius is the one who threatens to take away Jean Valjean's major source of meaning and happiness, his relationship with Cosette. Because of such a threat, Jean Valjean has come to hate Marius. Still, Jean Valjean, in an act of courage, kindness, and self-sacrifice, rescues the unconscious Marius via a daring escape through the sewers of Paris.

Much of the emotional power of this book derives from the moments at which Jean Valjean makes courageous ethical decisions. Yet the capacity for self-sacrifice carries a price for Jean Valjean. After Marius's rescue and the marriage of Marius and Cosette, Jean Valjean gradually becomes estranged from Marius, and thus from Cosette.

Marius, who is not aware of various details about Jean Valjean, doesn't know that his own life was saved by the great courage of Jean Valjean. Jean Valjean gradually becomes unwelcome as a visitor, and the pain of separation from his beloved Cosette hastens his fatal illness. The weakening of the bond with Cosette, which Jean Valjean had surely expected, renders his act of saving Marius even more self-sacrificial.

Jean Valjean makes an unfortunate decision in not simply telling Cosette and Marius the whole story of all that happened. He predicts that Marius would not believe him, because he is a convict. This prediction fails to take into account that Cosette has learned to trust Jean Valjean throughout her life. And if Cosette's trust were not sufficient to convince Marius, many of the details of Jean Valjean's story would be verifiable.

Jean Valjean's withholding this information makes for a heart-rending scene when Cosette and Marius finally find out the truth and reunite with Jean Valjean on his deathbed. But with open disclosure, Jean Valjean could perhaps have enjoyed a less dramatic but pleasant relationship with them into a comfortable old age.

Appendix 5: Activities for Psychological Skills

Writing on broad goals and methods

1. Writing assignment on skills, principles, attributes: Students are asked: What personal qualities, what psychological skills, or what character traits do you feel are important for a person to have, if the person is to be happy, successful, and good? What ethical principles or guidelines can you offer, to help people live a good life?

2. Writing assignment on methods of increasing skills: Suppose someone wants to get better at a certain skill, such as self-discipline or courage or kindness or concentrating for a long time. What methods can you think of, whereby the person can help himself or herself get more skilled?

Note: If students are able to answer these questions very articulately, they have a tremendous advantage over students who cannot do so. They have a sense of goals, and a sense of how to reach these goals. The song "What Are the Qualities," which lists the 16 skills and principles, gives one possible answer to the first question, and "OH RAM PRISM" (objective formation, hierarchy, relationship, attribution, modeling, practice, reinforcement, instruction, stimulus control, and monitoring) provides a possible answer to the second.

Activities on attributions

3. Lesson: explanation of attributions. When we have a bad habit, it's good to think of it as changeable, so that we can increase our morale to work on changing it. And when others have bad habits, it's good to think of those as possibly changeable too. The language we use makes a difference. If we say, "I am lazy," it sounds as though this is permanent. On the other hand, if we say, "If I am able to increase my work capacity, I'll be much more successful and happy," that way of thinking sets us up for improving ourselves. Or for a second example: If we think, about someone else, "He's a jerk," that tends to make us feel dislike of that person. But suppose we think, "If he learns to interrupt people less, be kinder, and handle not getting his way without getting so upset, he'll be much happier and will have more friends." This way of thinking will leave us more open to noticing any positive examples the person shows, and even reinforcing them.

4. Writing assignment on attributions: Please make up some examples of the types of attributions that might tend to demoralize ourselves and make us dislike others. Please translate each of these into attributions that give us energy to change in a positive way, and to reinforce others for their steps toward positive change.

Activities on reading the models and instructions

5. Reading exercise. Read many brief vignettes wherein characters model positive skills and principles, and identify which skills or principles are exemplified.

6. Reading exercise. Read nonfiction writing about psychological skills, such as *Programmed Readings For Psychological Skills*, and the other programmed courses, and answer the comprehension questions.

7. Listening exercise. Listen as one person (teacher, or student) reads to the rest of the group, materials about psychological skills, and answer the comprehension probes.

8. Alternate reading with programmed courses. Each student gets together with one other. They take turns reading out loud to each other each section of a programmed course, and they take turns being the first to answer the comprehension probe. The one who answers second reinforces the first if they agree on the right answer.

Activities on the twelve-thought classification

9. The Journey Story. Students listen while someone reads the story to the group, and answer the questions about what type of thought the person is thinking. Thus they become very familiar with the twelve-thought categorization. This story is part of *Programmed Readings for Psychological Skills*.

10. Discrimination exercise on the twelve thoughts. Given a situation and someone's thoughts in response to it, the student answers multiple choice questions about which of the twelve thoughts was exemplified in each question. The chapter on the twelve thought exercise in *Programmed Readings for Psychological Skills* is an example of this.

11. The twelve-thought exercise. Make up a situation, pleasant, unpleasant, or neutral. From the point of view of the person experiencing the situation, write an example of each of the twelve types of thoughts.

Note: Many people have been greatly helped by mastering the twelve thought categorization and then focusing on choosing the thoughts that are most useful in each given situation.

Activities on collecting positive models

12. The search for positive models. Search through literature, biography, history, film or television, poetry or song lyrics, or real-life experience for positive examples of psychological skills or character attributes. Please summarize what the situation was, and what the exemplar did, thought, and/or felt. Narrate the incident as vividly and specifically as you can. Tell what skill or principle or attribute the vignette exemplifies. What were the consequences to the doer, or to other people?

If you want to lift only a situation from some narrative and imagine someone responding to it in a good way, different from how the character in the original narrative did, that is fine! Just note how you are doing it.

13. The psychological skills book report. For a book that you have read, write a report that analyzes the actions of the characters. Which were positive models? Which were not? What consequences were there for the positive and negative models?

14. Positive models interview. Interview someone else, and find out what are the positive models that the person has done, that the person feels best about. In other words, what good decisions has the person made? Also: what actions have other people done that have most positively affected this person? How have other people been most helpful? Write up the results of this interview.

15. The celebrations diary. What is something that you have done, that you are glad to have done? Please describe very concretely the situation you were in, and your thoughts, emotions, and behaviors as you responded to the situation. Please identify the psychological skill or skills that this action was an example of.

16. The diary for celebration of others' actions. What has someone done that you feel grateful about? What skill or principle did the other person's behavior illustrate?

17. Writing skills stories. Please write a story that gives a positive model of a way of thinking, feeling, and/or

behaving. Please make up a comprehension question about what skill and principle the character's actions illustrate.

18. The picture-story activity. Pick at random a cut out picture from a magazine or a picture printed from the Internet, and write a skills story, using the picture as the illustration.

19. Writing a modeling play or story about a play plot. Use one of the plots listed in *Plays That Model Psychological Skills* and elaborate it into a full-blown narrative.

20. The psychological skills debate. Select a model that some people could view as positive, and others as negative. In writing, conduct a debate on whether the example is positive or negative, writing the arguments of both sides.

21. Teacher dictation of positive models. The teacher is provided a voice recorder. When the teacher sees a student doing a positive model, the teacher logs it away in memory, until a couple of minutes are available. At that time, the teacher picks up the voice recorder and, with the class listening, dictates a narrative of a student's carrying out of a positive model. (For suspense, the teacher might withhold the identity of the student and reveal it at the end.)

22. Transcribing of teacher dictations. Students take the teacher dictations of positive models and type them into

word processor files. Students are thus contributing to the positive model anthology, practicing keyboarding, spelling, and writing, and being exposed again to the positive model in question.

23. Editing the positive models anthology. Help to get an anthology of positive models into final form for publishing to other students.

24. Turning the positive models anthology into tests of reading comprehension. Make up typical reading comprehension test questions about entries in the positive models anthology.

25. Practicing reading comprehension, using the reading comprehension test version of the anthology. In class, or for homework, take the test.

23. Acting out examples from the positive models anthology. Pairs or groups of students briefly act out, for the rest of the students, positive modeling plays.

Persistence power activities

26. Practice of persistence power. Use the computer programs that are meant to measure persistence power, or tasks like them (where you can measure both objective work output and subjective feeling of persistence power) and see if the student can set a "personal best" record for persistence on one of the tasks. The tasks might include

vocabulary, spelling, typing, math facts, reading comprehension practice, math word problems, or others.

27. Graphing personal performance. The student enters on a graph the best performance of the day, for each of several days where performance is measured by frequency.

28. Work parties. Students are given the opportunity to do independent work with a partner, stopping occasionally to chat about how the work is going or anything else. Students try to socialize just enough to "recharge the batteries" and make the work party fun, but not so much that they detract from their productivity.

(More) Activities derived from exercises

29. Brainstorming options, orally. Students are given a one-person problem (individual decision choice point) or a two-person problem (joint decision choice point). The students hold up their hands and volunteer nonviolent options for the solutions of the problems. The class shoots for thinking of as many as possible of the options listed in a standard list.

30. Brainstorming options, in writing. Students write their list of options about a hypothetical problem they are assigned.

31. Creating more problem situations. Students orally, or in writing, add to the bank of problem-solving choice points and standard lists of options.

32. Generating specific choice points. The goal is to generate a large bank of situations to practice with.

    A. Self-discipline choice points
    B. Provocations (anger control choice points)
    C. Conflicts between people, to practice resolving
    D. Criticisms of one person by another, to practice responding to
    E. Fears (courage skill choice points)
    F. Social situations (friendship-building choice points)
    G. Kindness versus selfishness choice points
    H. Advice column problems and choice points (gleaned from a bank of questions posed to advice columnists)
    I. Real life problems for communities or nations to solve (gleaned from study of news media)
    J. Situations with an option to be considered, for practice in generating pros and cons for options.

33. The pros and cons exercise. For a situation and one option, list pros and cons. Variant: For a situation, and two or three options, write the advantages and disadvantages of each of the options. Use this analysis to justify a conclusion about which option is best.

34. The four thought exercise. For a given situation, write or say examples of the following types of thoughts: not

awfulizing, goal-setting, listing options and choosing, and celebrating your own choice.

35. SOIL ADDLEs. For any of the problems or choice points generated earlier, students write about the decision process, in detail. For interpersonal problems, the writer can imagine the results of information-gathering. For real-life problems of communities or nations, the students can research real-life information on the topic. In any case, they explain the situation, decide on objectives, get information, list options, explore advantages and disadvantages, and decide which option they think is best. In some cases they can imagine the decider doing the selected option and figuring out what, if anything, can be learned from the experience.

36. The tones of approval exercise, with the whole class, discriminating. The instructor writes on the board the phrases "large approval," "small to moderate approval," and "neutral." The instructor models different tones, and the students' jobs is to guess which tone the instructor was trying to model.

37. Tones of approval exercise, with the whole class, producing. The teacher puts on the board a set of phrases such as "Look at that," "Good job," "Look what you did," "That's interesting," and so forth. Students hold up their hands and say something with one of the tones of approval, and other students guess which of the tones the student was modeling.

38. Tones of approval exercise, in pairs. Students divide up into pairs to practice the tones of approval exercise, in which one says something, and the other guesses which tone he was trying to produce.

39. The reflections exercise, spoken, with the whole class. The instructor speaks, and every time the instructor stops, a student does a reflection. (I.e. a sentence starting "So you're saying _____," or "In other words, you're saying _____," or "What I hear you saying is _____," etc.

40. The reflections exercise, spoken, in pairs. The students pair up, and one is the speaker while the other is the reflector. Then they switch roles.

41. Written version of reflections exercise. The students make up dialogues in which one person speaks, and the other does a reflection every time the speaker stops speaking.

42. Which is the better reflection? The students are given examples of two different reflections to the same utterance. The task is to decide which of the two is "better" in that it more effectively paraphrases the speaker's meaning, without simply parroting it back. Sometimes a reflection is "worse" because it focuses on an unimportant part of what the person said rather than the part that makes the most difference.

43. Listening with four responses. The students use any of the formats used with the reflections exercise, only this time the listener, rather than simply doing reflections, varies the responses among reflections, facilitations (such as oh, I see, uh huh, yes, humh, etc.), follow-up questions, and positive feedback.

44. Social conversation role-play. The students use any of the formats used with the reflections exercise, only this time the roles of speaker and listener can switch ad lib in a fluid manner.

     A. Variation 1: the students are given hypothetical characters and a situation, and they act out the social conversation.
     B. Variation 2: the students are given hypothetical characters and a situation, and they compose in writing a social conversation.
     C. Variation 3: the students make up the situation and the characters, as well as the conversation that ensues.
     D. Variation 4: the students have social conversations without role-playing, but using their own personas.

45. Exercising as a way of restoring persistence power. Have students rate, on a scale of 0 to 10, their persistence power at this moment for seated academic work. The top of the scale means they're brimming with energy for more work. The bottom of the scale means they're so bored, tired, or restless that work is very difficult. Then they

exercise, and then fill out the scale again. Did exercise restore their persistence power? (Variation: students exercise, after which they do a few minutes of relaxation/biofeedback.)

Varieties of exercise:

A. Marching in place while doing arm motions against the resistance of the other hand.

B. Learning a dance step, and doing the dance step in place, to music.

C. Running.

D. Using a treadmill or other machine.

E. Going for a walk.

F. Doing a cooperative athletic activity, such as cooperative basketball.

G. Doing a traditional competitive athletic activity.

H. Doing a fitness test which gets compared to the student's past records, and possibly graphed. For example, stepping on and off a step, at a given pace, and counting pulse rates, per a standard protocol.

I. Doing some useful work that involves physical exertion.

J. Doing "aerobic chores": physical work, made to involve more physical exertion by running in place while doing it.

K. Bodyweight exercises or calisthenics.

Note: if students can be taught to notice restlessness in themselves and to "cure" this feeling by physical exercise, the long term health benefits may be tremendous.

46. Relaxation methods. The students, as a large group, experiment with two different methods of relaxation, and then write a brief report on what each of the methods was like for them. The methods might be muscle relaxation, imagery about a relaxing place, focusing on breathing (5 in and 5 out), imagery about kind acts, the good will meditation, the psychological skills meditation (the meditator goes through a list of positive skills and visualizes a positive model of each), repetition of a mantra such as the word "one," awareness of the contents of consciousness (or simply observing what comes to mind, without necessarily trying to influence it), and simple rest.

47. Biofeedback. The students use digital thermometers to measure fingertip temperature, or pulse oximeters to measure heart rate, or monitors of skin conductance level. They experiment with relaxation techniques they have learned, for two or three minutes or perhaps longer, and note the starting and ending level of the parameter. They ask the question of what technique leads most reliably to hand-warming. They also notice whether they are able, as a group, to increase the amount by which the parameters change, with repeated practice.

Note: There is reason to believe, from scores of studies on relaxation training, that if this skill could be successfully taught to students, many physical ailments, including many headaches, could be prevented; in addition, a great number of anxiety-related problems and probably anger-related problems could also be prevented.

48. Conflict-resolution role-play.

A. Written version. Students take one of the conflicts listed in A Programmed Course in Conflict-Resolution and Anger Control, and write a dialogue in which each person meets each of the 7 criteria for conflict-resolution. (Defining, Reflecting, Listing, Waiting, Advantages, Agreeing, Politeness, or Dr. L.W. Aap.)

B. Role-played version with instructor. A student and the instructor act out a conflict-resolution conversation in front of the class. When they are done, the class discusses which of the criteria were met and which were not.

C. Role-played in pairs. Students divide up in pairs and practice with a hypothetical conflict, aiming at meeting all 7 criteria.

D. Version wherein one character is using the 7 guidelines or criteria, despite the fact that the other is not. This is best done in the written version.

Note: I believe that if all school children were taught "to criterion" of excellence in the conflict-resolution role play, plus the four-thought exercise and fantasy rehearsals in response to provocations, the rate of violence in the world might be drastically improved. Anyone want to be on the forefront of doing this experiment?

49. Fantasy rehearsals. The student either takes a choice point situation that is assigned, or creates a choice point situation that is relevant to his or her own goals, and writes a fantasy rehearsal of the best possible response to the situation that the student can come up with. The format for fantasy rehearsals is to follow the STEBC: Situation, Thoughts, Emotions, Behaviors, and Celebration. The idea is to create what the student would LIKE to be able to do, not what the student is now in the habit of doing. In constructing thoughts, the twelve-thought categorization is very useful. In choosing emotions, it is good to consider emotions such as determination, curiosity, humility, pride, compassion, feeling cool and calculating, and others as modulators of anger, fear, and guilt. In choosing behaviors, it's good to draw upon the skills developed by the brainstorming options exercise and the pros and cons exercise.

Shaping and differential reinforcement

50. The shaping game. The instructor is shaper and a student is shapee, or vice versa, or two students are the players in front of the rest of the class. The goal behavior can be known to all but the shapee (written and shown while the shapee looks away, then removed from vision.) The shaper and shapee have the same goal, that the shapee will carry out the goal behavior. The shaper can provide clues only by giving positive reinforcement for something the shapee has already done.

51. Written follow-up to the shaping game.

A. Students write about a time when they have used internal self-shaping, while working for a goal.

B. Students imagine someone using internal self-shaping while working toward a goal, and write what the person's thoughts may be at different stages.

C. Students write about a time they have used shaping (or differential reinforcement) with another person in real life.

D. Students imagine someone using shaping (a.k.a. differential reinforcement) with another person, and write what this would look and sound like.

52. Parents as reinforcement officers.

A. a workshop, or several workshops, for parents can be conducted in person,

B. or some written material can be sent,

C. or phone conversations can be had with parents

so as to help parents learn how to use shaping and differential reinforcement with their children. This would cover the use of social reinforcers (emphasized) and tangible reinforcers (also sometimes useful).

53. Sending students "to the office" as reinforcement. When a student does something particularly good, the student gets sent to the principal's office, to talk with the principal or his/her agent about the positive model in

question. The principal can keep their own bank of positive models students have carried out.

54. The four R's in place of punishment. Students write stories in which someone does something wrong or mistaken, and then takes responsibility, makes restitution, does some good redecision about what would be better to do the next time, and does fantasy or role-played rehearsals of the improved pattern.

55. Award ceremonies. If a "ranks and challenges" program is instituted for psychological skills, students at ceremonies are given certificates or patches recognizing their achievement.

56. Students' recognition of one another. Students periodically report the exemplary acts that their fellow students have carried out.

Goal attainment and self-discipline

57. Goal-setting: discrimination practice. The instructor provides students with pairs of goals, and asks students to discuss, or write about, which goal they believe will *usually* provide the higher return for the work invested. For example, one person wants to own a very expensive pair of shoes, and another person wants to teach someone else to read. What are the differences between these? Or for another example, one person wants to be known as the best fighter on his block, and another wants to get above a certain score on a standardized test. Although it's

impossible to say that some goals are always better than others, can students make up goals where one is *usually* a better one to pursue than the other?

58. Goal-setting: The student chooses. The student writes about the answers to the following questions. What is a goal that the student really wants to adopt in real life? Can this goal be expressed very specifically, so that it will be possible to know whether the goal has been met or not)? By what time would the student like to meet the goal? Is it a worthy goal? Is it in keeping with one or more of the core skills or principles or values that the student has adopted?

59. Student self-monitoring, using the psychological skills inventory. Frequently, a worthy goal is to increase one's productivity, joyousness, kindness, honesty, fortitude, decision-making, anger control, respectful talk, and so forth. If students repeatedly rate themselves in these skills, they may be more likely to adopt improvement in one or more of these as a goal. There are versions of the questionnaire that ask, "How skilled are you at each of these," and that ask, "How much do you want to improve at each of these?" Both questions are worth asking periodically.

60. The internal sales pitch. Given a goal that the student has chosen, the student writes about the answer to the question, "Why should I work on this? What payoffs could come from achieving this goal?"

61. The plan for the goal. Given a goal that the student has chosen, the student writes an answer to the question, "What is your plan for achieving this goal? What activities will you do? How much time will you put into this? What obstacles may come up? What's your plan for overcoming them? Who will help you achieve this goal? In what ways? What's your timeline? How likely do you think your plan is to work?"

62. The self-discipline choice points for a goal. Given a goal that the student has chosen, the student lists the choice points that are important ones in achieving the goal. For example, for a student who wants to get an A in a course, a choice point might be, "I have an assignment to do for this course. I feel like trying to watch television while doing the assignment."

63. Fantasy rehearsals of positive responding to choice points for a goal. Given a goal that the student has chosen, and choice points the student has made up, the student writes fantasy rehearsals of positive responses to the choice points listed.

64. Celebrations of work toward a goal. Given a goal the student has chosen, the student reports on celebrations relevant to this goal, i.e. specific positive actions that advance the cause of the goal.

65. Monitoring of progress toward a goal. Given a goal the student has chosen, the student writes progress reports,

detailing how progress toward the goal is being measured and what the measures are revealing so far.

66. Report on a short-term self-discipline challenge, or a resolution. As part of the student's attainment of the goal, the student resolves to do something that can be done at one particular sitting. For example, if the goal is a good grade in a course, the student may resolve to review for at least half an hour tonight. If the goal is getting in good physical condition, the student may resolve to do aerobic exercise for at least half an hour tonight. If the goal is to get better organized, the student may resolve to work for at least half an hour on organizing his or her workplace at home, tonight. The student writes down what the resolution is, and why it is worthwhile to do.

The next day, the teacher hands out the resolutions the students turned in the previous day, and asks the students to write about what happened. The teacher makes it clear that the student can be totally honest if the resolution was not kept, because we can learn from resolutions not kept as well as those that were kept. Was the resolution too ambitious? Did some unforeseen circumstance arise? Or was this resolution prey to the universal human tendency to find it more difficult to keep resolutions than to make them? On the other hand, if the resolution was kept, what factors helped the student keep it? Did the student use self-reinforcement, so as to make keeping the next resolution easier?

Useful work

67. Becoming conscious of a distinction. In this activity, the students discuss or write about the distinction between work that is designed to prove one's potential to do useful work, and useful work itself. Both can be very important. For example, preparation for the SAT test is meant to prove that you can do the work of college, at least some of which is usually meant to prepare you to do directly useful work. Shoveling snow or teaching another student or helping your grandmom get to the bathroom are directly useful work, and having a career as a janitor, teacher, doctor, president, fruit-picker, business manager, or many others are also directly useful work.

68. Useful work assignments. Students are allowed to volunteer for useful work assignments that foster the goals of the school: for example transcribing teachers' dictations of positive models, scanning, cleaning, helping with repairs, and so forth.

69. The useful work diary. Students either write about, or hold up their hands and tell about, directly useful work they have done or have seen others do.

Tutoring other students

70. Reading the instructions. Students read instructions on how to be a good tutor, and they take reading comprehension tests on the instructional material. They continue this activity to the criterion of mastery of the material.

71. Role-playing of tutoring activities, in front of the class. After reading about how to do a certain activity, students preparing to be tutors practice in role-playing with the instructor, in front of the class. The instructor gives feedback that will be useful to all.

72. Role-playing of tutoring activities, divided up into pairs or triplets. Students practice tutoring activities with one another. When they are divided into triplets, one person is the tutor, the second is the student, and the third is the monitor, who gives feedback on how the activity was carried out. A checklist or rating scale should be available to the monitor. The rating scale should always include "tones of approval." The role-played tutor may rate himself or herself before hearing the tutor's feedback. The instructor "floats" during these role-played sessions and listens to parts of each.

73. Practice of tutoring, with real students. After practicing thoroughly, the tutor begins work with a real student. Other students monitor the session, using a checklist. The instructor floats.

74. Review of tutoring videos. Certain tutoring sessions are video recorded and reviewed in front of the group. The instructor gives feedback, using the rating scale. The tutor himself or herself may want to self-monitor first.

75. Writing about tutoring sessions. From recorded transcripts, the instructor, together with the students, select instructive moments that illustrate good or bad choices on the part of the tutor. These are transcribed by students. The students, with the help of the instructor, write about why the tutor's technique was exemplary, or a "learn from the mistake" example. This is a high level activity, which cumulates into instructive and helpful manuals for tutors.

76. Self-monitoring of sessions. After the session, the tutor writes a brief report of what the goals of the session were, whether the goals were achieved, what the celebrations are, what the learnings for next time are, and how desirable in all is it that the techniques of this session are repeated in the next session.

77. Outcome monitoring of tutoring. The tutor gives a reading recognition test to the student of reading, for example, and scores the test. Or the tutor gives a test of math facts to the student of math, or dictates spelling words to the learner of spelling. The tutor and the student graph the results of repeated testing on the learner's graph.

Activities with music

78. Discrimination exercise, with song lyrics. In a class discussion, the instructor presents lyrics to various songs. The students are asked to comment upon the level of psychological skill, ethical attitudes, or positive values reflected or not reflected by the song lyrics. Which skills, principles, or attributes do these song lyrics give positive

or negative examples of? After discussing this, the students may be asked to write about this question, with other examples of song lyrics.

79. Variant of discrimination exercise with song lyrics. Students are given blank scrap paper and markers. After listening to song lyrics read aloud, they rate the degree of psychological skill or ethics reflected in the lyrics they heard, on a scale of 1 to 10, independently, and then they simultaneously raise their cards and show them to everyone else. In discussion, they explain the reason for their choices.

80. The quest for positive song lyrics. Students search for songs that model positive psychological skills. They bring in the lyrics, written down, and read them clearly to the rest of the class. If the class agrees that the lyrics are worthy, the song is added to the bank of positive modeling songs.

81. Group listening to positive modeling songs. At spare moments, the lyrics to positive modeling songs are projected upon a screen, and the song is played. This activity may be combined with exercising with dance steps.

82. Group singing of positive modeling songs. Everyone simply sings the songs, with or without instrumental accompaniment.

83. Learning harmony parts to modeling songs. If the teacher can find harmony parts written, or write them, or record them, or find them recorded, they can be taught to the students.

84. Performing of harmony on modeling songs.
    A. The whole group can harmonize.
    B. Pairs or trios or quartets of students can perform modeling songs, with harmonizing if possible.

85. Recording modeling songs. Students who do well enough on modeling songs make audio or video recordings to add to the bank of positive models.

86. Students teach instrument lessons for others. Those who know how to play an instrument give individual lessons to those who want to learn to play. Faculty can help the student-teacher decide what point on the hierarchy of difficulty is appropriate, what activities and challenges should be done, how much to ask the learner to use other-directed activity versus self-directed activity, and so forth. Ideally, the repetitive practice necessary for learning an instrument can become fun, because of a partner who supplies reinforcement.

Activities for art

87. Repeatable art assignment: produce whatever work of art you think is worthwhile to do, and if you choose, tell about what you have made.

88. Stories from the bank of positive models are illustrated by students. Some of the illustrated stories are scanned into a computer and published as illustrated modeling stories.

89. Creation of animations. Computer programs for animation are used to create animated plays that model psychological skills.

90. Creation of pictures for storytelling. The artists create pictures of people in situations that can stimulate a variety of different stories about the people or events in the picture.

91. Creation of relaxing images. A relaxation method is to imagine settings and/or characters that are beautiful, cozy, safe, inviting, comforting – artists may create an anthology of these to use in relaxation/meditation practice.

Activities using drama

92. Composing plays that model psychological skills. Students write plays modeling psychological skills, some of which are designed for two people to act out (either with only two characters, or one or more of the actors taking on the part of another character at some point), and some of which are designed for a small group of people. Students look at models of how to write stage directions and screenplays in preparation for this.

93. Acting out plays that model psychological skills. Students act out plays that have been composed, either

reading the scripts verbatim, or getting the plot in mind and improvising the lines without looking at the script.

94. Improvising specific plots from very general plots. Students draw general plot outlines – for example, "One person has a problem because something that they are using doesn't work right. The other person helps them out." They get up and act out a little play making this specific – for example, the first person's lawnmower won't work, and the second person happens to have a very hungry goat who would like to eat the first person's grass. Or the first person's car breaks down, in the middle of a terrible snowstorm, and the second person, who lives nearby, lets the person go inside and get warm until help comes for the car.

95. Improvising social conversation between various toy people or animals. Students randomly pick toy characters, and they have them conduct a "getting to know the other" conversation.

96. Dramatic play with toy people and props. Pairs of students go to stations where there are toy characters and props such as houses, barns, tractors, airports, planes, etc. (no guns). They improvise dramatic play with each other. Teachers observe parts of the play, and record and report to the whole group the positive models of psychological skills they saw enacted during the plays. (This brand of improvisational drama is unfortunately considered in general youth culture to be too "babyish" for children of a

certain age, despite the fact that doing it well is an extremely challenging and creative activity.)

More activities for school culture

97. Self-monitoring of school culture. Students fill out questionnaires and write narratives about how successfully the school culture promotes the skills, principles, and attributes that form the core values. What aspects are most successful in doing this? What suggestions are there on how to do this better?

98. Self-monitoring regarding bullying. Students fill out questionnaires about the issue of bullying. To what extent do they feel that they have been bullied, or have they bullied others? To what extent is there a "conspiracy of silence," an unwritten rule that you can't talk about being bullied? Versus how much is bullying behavior very open to discussion with parents and/or teachers and/or counselors and other staff? To what extent does the rule of law versus vigilante justice prevail in this school? How kind is the interpersonal climate of the school, as perceived by each student?

99. Pledges, affirmations, readings. There are public displays of the core values of the school. There are many times when the core values are read or recited aloud by groups.

100. Public speaking. Students and faculty members give speeches to assembled groups having to do with the encouragement of psychological skills in the school.

101. Monitoring of faculty tones of voice. Faculty help each other monitor their own tones of approval and disapproval. To what extent do teachers' tones of voice model the sort of emotional tone we wish students to adopt?

102. The social-emotional-behavioral part of the report card. The faculty construct a rating scale or form for the report card that corresponds to the core values of the school, whereby it can be communicated to parents and to the student how well the student is doing and how much progress is being made in these skill areas. If possible, studies are done regarding the reliability and validity of these ratings.

103. Further parent education. Furnishing, for parents who desire it, materials on psychological skill instruction, so that the parent can reinforce the efforts of the school, and ideally the whole family can work on the skills along with the student.

Activities for nonviolence

104. Study of nonviolence and its heroes

105. Analysis of the story of the violent hero

106. Adding to, revising, publishing the bank of provocations (including conflicts, criticisms...)

107. Dr. L.W. Aap conflict-resolution and joint decision-making dialogues

108. Composing options for provocations (Ida Craft is mnemonic for classes of nonviolent responses)

109. Composing options for responses to criticism (T Paarisec is mnemonic for options for responses to criticism

110. Twelve-thought exercise and four-thought exercise with provocations

111. Analysis of real-life conflicts

112. Celebrations exercise with real-life joint decision-making

113. Envisioning a nonviolent society

Activity for mental-health-friendly environments

114. Writing, thinking, discussing what aspects of an environment make it mental-health-friendly, how to achieve those conditions, how to be agents of creating those conditions.

Alphabetical Index